But God Meant It for Good

Lessons From the Life of Joseph

RONNIE MCBRAYER

Smyth & Helwys Publishing, Inc.
6316 Peake Road
Macon, Georgia 31210-3960
1-800-747-3016
©2008 by Smyth & Helwys Publishing
All rights reserved.
Printed in the United States of America.

The paper used in this publication meets the minimum requirements of
American National Standard for Information Sciences—
Permanence of Paper for Printed Library Materials.
ANSI Z39.48–1984. (alk. paper)

Library of Congress Cataloging-in-Publication Data

McBrayer, Ronnie.
But God meant it for good : lessons from the life of Joseph / by Ronnie
McBrayer.
p. cm.
ISBN 978-1-57312-504-8 (alk. paper)
1. Joseph (Son of Jacob) I. Title.

BS580.J6M383 2008
222'.11092--dc22
2007045035

Contents

Acknowledgments

Thomas Carlyle said, "Every noble work is at first impossible." Recognizing all those who have had a part in bringing this book into print may be a noble task. Certainly it is impossible. But here is a start.

Thank you to the congregation of Seaside Chapel, and to Pastor Jeff Miller especially, for giving me the flexibility of time to complete this project. I could not have done it without your partnership in ministry. It is a joy to serve with you all.

To Gwen Break and her staff: Holding my feet to the deadline fire each week has made me more disciplined and intentional. Thank you.

Gratitude galore to the congregation of Blackwood Springs Church who first "heard" this book in a series of talks years ago. Your immediate feedback in those days has shaped the final product.

There are supporters too numerous to name who have played an integral part of this project and most everything in which I'm involved. They have given financially, emotionally, and prayerfully—and with generous hearts. Great is your reward.

Jim and Amelia Gibby, Chris and Sharlene Hale, Phil and Leanne Amico, Kathy Ault—Your friendships are the medicine of life.

Blayze, Bryce, and Braden, my chosen sons. Boys, I thank you for your patience, though the answer to your question "What are you writing about?" is still "I don't really know."

Finally, and most importantly, I thank my wife, Cindy. God gave me the best when he gave me you.

Introduction

Example is the school of mankind, and they will learn at no other.
—Edmund Burke

I was first introduced to Joseph in my childhood. He burst onto the flannel graph board of my Sunday school classroom, his infamous coat of many colors flapping in the Palestinian breeze. For decades now he has intrigued me, encouraged me, and challenged me.

His story has been enough to capture my imagination as a child and enough to sustain my faith as an adult. If you have not taken the time to get to know Joseph, then let me introduce you to him and his family.

What will you find in the story of my friend Joseph? A great deal, to say the least, for his adventures are enough to fill several lifetimes. Jealousy, deception, injustice, forgiveness, redemption—all of this jumps from the pages as Joseph's life takes more twists and turns than a modern-day roller coaster.

We read about his dysfunctional family and feel the corkscrew turns of deceit and rivalry. In the conspiracy of his brothers against him, the G-force seems almost crushing. We experience with him a crippling, sudden stop when he is alone and abandoned in a Middle Eastern prison. Then the speed in which he rises to the seat of world power takes the air from our lungs. Through it all, and sometimes in spite of it, God faithfully brings Joseph's life to its intended destiny.

I hope Joseph will bring to you what he has brought to me: Reflection. Inspiration. Spiritual transformation. Encouragement to see the larger picture.

Most of all, I seek for you, the reader, identification with the story of God. That is, I seek for you to see, hear, and feel yourself in these often overlooked pages of the Old Testament, and then to translate Joseph's experiences into reality; that is, to create points of reference and personal conversion.

You will find much in the story of Joseph, but the most important and surprising thing you will find is yourself. Maybe you will discover a clue to what God is doing in your life.

I offer a word of warning as we begin: This is not a "how-to" book. You will find no keys for successful living or catchy alliterated principles to revolutionize your life. There are no miraculous prayers or step-by-step solutions to solve your most pressing problems. In fact, there is more paradox and mystery in Joseph's story than I am sometimes comfortable with.

Still, the journey of his life is a beautiful, sometimes tragic narrative that continues to form and speak to us today. It speaks especially to those of us who are

- trying to make sense of what is going on in our lives.
- wondering what God is doing in some faraway heaven.
- feeling that the chaos of life has little or no meaning.

If any of this describes you—like this baffling though marvelous story of Joseph—then this book was written with you in mind.

A word of thanks: This book is based largely on a series of talks I first delivered in autumn 2002 at Blackwood Springs Baptist Church in Calhoun, Georgia. I owe a great debt of gratitude to Jane Ellen Fite, who preserved those talks and returned them to me at the most opportune time.

May the encouragement I have received from the life and story of Joseph be yours as well.

My Twelve Sons

Look at the families in the Bible. . . . There are more nut-cake families and fruit-cake families than there are angel-food-cake families.

—Leonard Sweet

Ruth and Elliot Handler birthed their baby girl into a world full of expectation. As they gazed at their tiny and exceptionally beautiful daughter, marveling at her blonde hair and blue eyes, her parents knew she was destined for greatness. She did not disappoint.

Blossoming into nothing less than a Madison Avenue sensation, she began a decades-long domination of the fashion and entertainment worlds. At the tender age of ten she had already earned more than five hundred million dollars, and even today there seems to be no end to her popularity, as she makes nearly two billion dollars a year.

Magazines, books, websites, movies, television, DVDs—every media outlet in existence—continue their love affair with this American beauty. Other siblings have joined the family, as beautiful and flawless as their older sister, but none have reached her iconic status.

This fair lady has visited 90 percent of American girls' homes in the last forty years and has created and recreated herself for more than 140 nations and people groups. Always beautiful, wearing one of the thousands of outfits from her closet, rich and trendy on the cusp of today's fashion, wildly successful in every one of the nearly eighty careers she has pursued, and forever the center of attention surrounded by a smiling cluster of family and friends—she is absolutely perfect.

While she is sometimes maligned and often parodied, she holds fiercely to that place of perfection, inspiring millions of young girls to become all they can be, inspiring millions to become more like her.

She is Miss Barbie Millicent Roberts; better known simply as Barbie.

The only problem, of course, is that she is a fantasy. She is a toy—a mass of injected-molding vinyl. Certain Barbies can be worth tens of thousands of dollars, but she more often than not ends up naked and dismembered on the floors of older brothers' bedrooms.

Barbie is a reflection of our desires. She has none of her own. This was, after all, Ruth Handler's motivation in creating her. Ruth watched her real daughter playing as a child and saw the future. Her daughter, all daughters, needed more than a baby doll that did little more than arouse maternal desires. They needed a doll—a person—to inspire and challenge them to become something out of their wildest dreams. Thus Barbie was born.

As adults we learn that carefully crafted idealism and hardened reality don't always meet. Most of us do not lead Ken and Barbie lives. We feel a lot more at home with Homer and Marge Simpson.

Still, we sometimes bring those Ken and Barbie idealisms to the Bible and its characters. I grew up in the church with these Bible characters as my heroes. I was taught that I could slay the giant like David. I could have mountain-moving faith like Abraham. I could call down fire from heaven like Elijah.

Much later, I learned that for all their glorious deeds, these heroes of mine had tons of baggage too. David the giant killer was also David the adulterer and an accomplice to murder. Abraham, the father of faith for Jews, Muslims, and Christians alike, could dissolve into a compulsive liar if the situation so demanded. Elijah, defiant warrior of Mount Carmel, once became so emotionally and spiritually despondent that he nearly committed suicide. All these biblical champions of faith were inspirational, yes, but also very human. They were real people not unlike you or me.

These same idealistic projections have been laid alongside today's families. Christians, evangelicals in particular, seem to have an obsession with the "biblical family." I don't think this term means exactly what some think it does.

I know what many people intend by the idea. By applying biblical principles, Christians could (and the implication is *should*) produce the ideal "biblical" family: a strong, spiritual father; a faithful, loving mother; and two-and-a-half obedient, always compliant children.

The word "biblical" is used synonymously with "traditional," as many Christians pine for a return to the days of the Cleaver family. Again, the only problem is that this too is a fantasy, about as credible as a television sitcom. We may be inspired to reach for such an ideal as the "traditional" family, but when we do we usually find frustration and failure. Sure, a few pull it off. Most of us do not. Further, the "biblical" family, as it is commonly referred to, is not a valid example toward which to aspire—shocking, I know.

My family may be a bit screwy, but I wouldn't trade it for Adam and Eve's where one brother killed the other. I wouldn't switch places with Hosea whose wife was the village prostitute. Why swap my one set of in-laws for Solomon's seven hundred?

Recently I read that the largest Protestant seminary in North America is beginning a certificate program in "Christian Homemaking." This graduate school is launching a rigorous thirty-hour program to train women to wax floors, prepare meals, make their family's clothes, and meet the needs of their hard-working, breadwinning husbands. This is, according to the seminary's president, a woman's place.[1]

I don't think this return to the "biblical" model of marriage is as desirable as it might seem. Most marriages during biblical days were arranged. The new wife, typically about fifteen years of age or younger, was given to a man twice her age. Love was neither a requirement nor an expectation. The woman was a piece of property, serving as an economic asset at worst and a producer of meals and male heirs at best. If she failed at either of these tasks, replacing her was as easy as the waving of a hand. The woman had no rights and no legal recourse for defense.

Further, a man having multiple partners, in marriage or with mistresses, was entirely acceptable. Many of the great saints of old practiced polygamy. It is a well-established biblical pattern. I wonder if this seminary will succeed in correcting this glaring violation in the biblical order.

Additionally, who really needs a marriage certificate? Why secure a judge or a justice of the peace to square the deal? While marriage covenants are as old as time itself, the civil marriage ceremony didn't become popular until after the Council of Trent. Only then did the Catholic church declare marriage a sacrament. Civil weddings certified by the government, as we know them today, are a recent invention of post-Reformation, modern, secular Europe—not the Bible.

Most of the families found in the Bible are more dysfunctional than my own. Maybe that is all the more reason to be drawn to these examples and to find in their failures and regrets the seeds of redemption and grace.

So it is with the family of Joseph.

Genesis 37 opens with these words: "This is the account of Jacob and his family." Nonetheless, it is Jacob's son, Joseph, who will occupy center stage of this drama for the next fifteen chapters, some one hundred years, even after Jacob passes from the scene. Yet, those opening words of the chapter provide the context for Joseph's life—that of a disjointed, combative family with nothing marking it as a remarkable example to follow.

Consider the players: one manipulative, scheming father; four jealous, competing wives and mothers; twelve brawling sons and an untold number of daughters; plus the surge of grandchildren and great-grandchildren—all living under the same canopy.

Certainly this is a biblical family—there it is in the text—but "traditional" is not the first word that comes to mind. Impaired or wrecked, maybe, but not traditional. This family is a seething cauldron of anger and resentment that boils over more regularly than the family's porridge bowl. We should not be surprised. A quick look at the patriarch Jacob helps explain how the family arrived at this juncture.

Jacob was the second son of Isaac and grandson of the great Abraham. As a young man, and with the assistance of his amorous mother, he slyly obtained his brother's birthright. The birthright was a special blessing designated in ancient times for the firstborn son. Jacob then duped his old, blind, and dying father into giving him that blessing. He is aptly named.

Jacob, in the original Hebrew language, means "heel-grabber," or "one who causes others to stumble." He earned this name on the day of his birth, clinging to his twin brother's heel as they burst from the womb, and he lived up to that name the rest of his life.

Without a doubt mothers warned their daughters to stay clear of this silver-tongued pretender, for he could talk a young lady into almost anything. Fathers told their sons to avoid any dealings with him, because he did not lose to anyone. And those who transacted business with him had better get the details in writing in the presence of their attorney.

Jacob always found a way to get what he wanted even if a violation of conscience and a flexing of the rules of engagement were involved. Every time he said, "My name is Jacob," he was making a confession about his life, his behavior, and the choices he had made.

As a young man, Jacob fell madly in love with his cousin Rachel, daughter of Laban. He asked for her hand in marriage. Laban was willing to arrange the marriage on one condition: Jacob would work on Laban's farm for seven years.

It was a proposition not many young men would have been willing to accept, but Jacob agreed. The Bible says, "So Jacob worked seven years to pay for Rachel. But his love for her was so strong that it seemed to him but a few days" (Gen 29:20).[2] Eventually the wedding feast was thrown, the family celebrated, and the newlywed couple consummated their marriage. On the morning following the wedding, however, it was not Rachel in Jacob's bed. It was her older, less attractive sister, Leah. Jacob was outraged.

> But when Jacob woke up in the morning—it was Leah! "What have you done to me?" Jacob raged at Laban. "I worked seven years for Rachel! Why have you tricked me?"
>
> "It's not our custom here to marry off a younger daughter ahead of the firstborn," Laban replied. "But wait until the bridal week is over, then we'll give you Rachel, too—provided you promise to work another seven years for me." (Gen 29:25-27)

Jacob, remarkably, agreed. What choice did he have? His heart was bound to the beautiful Rachel. He loved her like no other. So, after fourteen years of difficult labor, victimized by a bit of heel grabbing himself, he finally had the woman he loved. But he also had her scorned older sister, and the rivalry was nearly unbearable.

That rivalry intensified all the more when children were added to the muddle. Note the meanings of some of the names of the unloved Leah's children: Reuben, "the Lord has seen my misery; surely my husband will love me now"[3]; Simeon, "the Lord heard that I am not loved"[4]; Levi, "At last my husband will become attached to me."[5]

Rachel, unable to achieve a pregnancy and thus unable to compete with her sister, gave her own servant Bilhah to Jacob as a wife and surrogate mother. The names of Bilhah's sons, named by Rachel, are equally as revealing: Dan, "God has vindicated me"[6]; Naphtali, "I have had a great struggle with my sister and I have won."[7]

Leah, now barren herself, refused to be outdone. She offered to Jacob her maidservant, Zilpah. He took her into his bed as well, and the sons she produced were named Gad, "what good fortune,"[8] and Asher, "how happy I am."[9]

Finally, Rachel, the true love of Jacob despite his three other wives, was able to conceive and birth a son. The firstborn of the beloved Rachel was Joseph. Rachel would give Jacob one more son. Dying in childbirth, she gave life to Benjamin, and the tumultuous family of Jacob was complete.[10]

It should come as no surprise, then, given a bit of history, that this would be a family rife with conflict.

Upon Rachel's death it seems that the love Jacob had for her fell squarely on the shoulders of Joseph, her firstborn son. The burden of this love is most noticeable in that famous gift, the coat of many colors: "Jacob loved Joseph more than any of his other children because Joseph had been born to him in his old age. So one day Jacob had a special gift made for Joseph—a beautiful robe" (Gen 37:3).

This Technicolor Dream Coat was not the cloak of a common shepherd, though sheep herding is how the family sustained itself.[11] No, this was the garment of a prince, the coat of a king. It was obvious even to a family outsider that Joseph was the son of choice.

Jacob was playing favorites with his children, even as his own mother had favored him, and this favoritism incited the wrath of the brothers against Joseph. Note their animosity: "But his brothers hated Joseph because their father loved him more than the rest of them" (Gen 37:4). "His brothers . . . hated him" (Gen 37:8). "His brothers were jealous of Joseph" (Gen 37:11).

The only thing more celebrated than Joseph's coat, and the only thing more irritating to his brothers, was his magnificent dreams.

In Genesis 37:5-11 we read,

One night Joseph had a dream, and when he told his brothers about it, they hated him more than ever. "Listen to this dream," he said. "We were out in the field, tying up bundles of grain. Suddenly my bundle stood up, and your bundles all gathered around and bowed low before mine!" His brothers responded, "So you think you will be our king, do you? Do you actually think you will reign over us?" And they hated him all the more because of his dreams and the way he talked about them.

Soon Joseph had another dream, and again he told his brothers about it. "Listen, I have had another dream," he said. "The sun, moon, and eleven stars bowed low before me!"

This time he told the dream to his father as well as to his brothers, but his father scolded him. "What kind of dream is that?" he asked. "Will your mother and I and your brothers actually come and bow to the ground before you?" But while his brothers were jealous of Joseph, his father wondered what the dreams meant.

Certainly it was not Joseph's fault for dreaming. Such dreams apparently ran in the family. In a case of the fruit not falling far from the tree, it was Jacob, Joseph's father, who dreamed of angels climbing and descending the stairway to heaven. But as a teenager at the time, Joseph lacked the maturity to be quiet about his dreams.

The author of the text portrays him with a patronizing tone as he speaks to his brothers and even his father about the pictures that soared through his head at night. He couldn't even finish his corn flakes in the morning before blurting out every painful detail. He used his dreams as barbs in the already unstable relationship with his brothers.

These brothers, all but Benjamin much older than he, could stand very little of this. Here he was, the baby boy of the family, favored and protected by their father, dreaming these colossal dreams of ruling over the family and speaking of such things with that bright jacket tossed over his shoulders like some prancing monarch. He didn't know when to shut up, and it would cost him years of his life.

DreX in the Morning is a popular radio show on the airways of Chicago, Illinois. You'll find the typical morning madness there: talk, music, traffic reports, news. And confessions.

Callers dial in to confess their latest infidelities, pranks, and road rage. They do so mainly for entertaining rather than atoning purposes. But one morning a caller confessed a little too much. I couldn't help chuckling over his bold foolishness.

His name was simply "D," and he bragged that he and a number of associates had robbed a Twin Cities Federal Bank in Chicago almost a year earlier. He gave intricate details of the whole affair down to the exact amount stolen: $81,000. He even boasted of going immediately to Michigan Avenue and purchasing a Louis Vuitton wallet—paying in cash—to celebrate the accomplishment.

The radio personalities may not have taken the call seriously, but a Twin Cities bank employee driving into work that morning heard the tale and recognized it as the holdup that had indeed occurred at her bank months earlier. She immediately called the authorities.

It didn't take long for the FBI to trace the call back to a cell phone belonging to a Mr. Randy Washington, age twenty-four. He was quickly arrested and charged with the crime. There had been no leads in the investigation until that one blabbering phone call.

In an official statement (understatement may be more accurate), an assistant U.S. attorney said, "The details he provided were incredibly helpful in moving this investigation forward." Upon arrest, the FBI found a Louis Vuitton wallet in "D's" hip pocket. Inside was a receipt showing he had in fact paid with cash.[12]

While Joseph's loose talk about his ambitious dream life would seal his fate, and while he may have stoked the flames of brotherly hostility with that talk, he did not light those fires. Remember, this is Jacob's account, not Joseph's. This dysfunctional family was largely Jacob's responsibility.

It is interesting that, for a man so shrewd in his dealings with others, Jacob showed little of that same skill regarding his own family. He plunged ahead with multiple marriages, showed obvious favoritism with his children, and did little to alleviate the rivalries that tore the family tent to shreds. It was not Joseph who created the hazardous world into which he was born, but Joseph had no choice other than to live in it.

Are we any different? We did not pick our families, but we have no choice other than to live with them. We are not responsible for the inheritance of poverty or incest or addiction, but for many these are ever-present actualities. We did not stuff the family closet with its secrets and skeletons. They were there long before we arrived.

We did not intentionally plan for a divorce, but it intruded as the unwelcome guest crashing our marital party. We did not wish for our partner to be unfaithful or to become abusive or for our children to live rebellious, hurtful lives. We could not have anticipated the sickness or tragedy that took our loved one away far too soon. But these things happen.

Still, there is hope. If the story of Jacob, Joseph, and this family ended abruptly here in Genesis 37, our only conclusion would be that the family was headed toward disintegration. There had been too much pain; too much rivalry; too much hostility. It was more than they could overcome. Even so, God was at work in the chaos and hardness of Jacob's household.

Consider this unexpected turn of events:

> A rock hound named Rob Cutshaw owns a little roadside shop outside Andrews, North Carolina. Like many in the trade, he hunts for rocks, then sells them to collectors or jewelry makers. He knows enough about rocks to decide which to pick up and sell, but he's no expert. He leaves the appraising of his rocks to other people.

As much as he enjoys the work, it doesn't always pay the bills. He occasionally moonlights, cutting wood to help put bread on the table. While on a dig twenty years ago, Rob found a rock he described as "purdy and big." He tried unsuccessfully to sell the specimen and kept the rock under his bed or in his closet. He guessed the blue chunk could bring as much as five hundred dollars, but he would have taken less if something urgent came up like paying his power bill. That's how close Rob came to hawking for a few hundred dollars what turned out to be the largest, most valuable sapphire ever found.

The blue rock that Rob had abandoned to the darkness of a closet is now known as "The Star of David" sapphire. It weighs nearly a pound, and appraised for more than $2.75 million. Only the expert eye could estimate its worth.[13]

Though immature and misunderstood as a young man, Joseph would indeed become the figure of his dreams. God knew his actual worth and saw far more than a bratty kid in a shiny coat. God would use Joseph to save the lives of the entire family and preserve the future of what would become a great nation.

The hard-boiled hate of his brothers would dissolve into a puddle of remorse and grief. Restoration, seemingly impossible and a lifetime in the making, would finally come. God brought beauty from the burnt ashes of this family as only God can. And yes, God can do the same even for us living in the shattered families of the twenty-first century.

If you think your family is beyond redemption and grace, think again. God is still at work. He can see what we and our families are truly made of, and he can bring the good seed buried deep within us to maturity.

And by the way, after more than forty years together, in the throes of midlife crisis, Barbie kicked Ken to the curb. Though jilted and heartbroken, Ken is determined to win her back. But it makes you think. Maybe even Barbie isn't as perfect as we thought.[14]

Questions for Reflection

1. Much energy is put into making Christian families traditional. I propose that the "traditional" American family does not necessarily equal a biblical family. Do you agree or disagree? Why?

2. Why do you think Jacob so favored Joseph? Have you ever experienced this in your own family? If so, how has this affected your closest relationships?

3. Why did Joseph speak so loosely about his dreams? Could Joseph have handled himself more appropriately?

4. Joseph and his brothers would finally experience a seemingly impossible restoration. Is there someone with whom you wish you could enjoy a restored relationship? What keeps you from restoring that relationship?

5. Though you may not be responsible for much of the dysfunction in your family, you may still have to bear the consequences. Have you found this to be unfair? What would you change about your family if you could?

6. Do you tend to see the characters of the Bible as better or holier than you? Why or why not?

Notes

[1] Bob Allen, "Baptist Seminary Offers Degree in Homemaking for Pastors' Wives," 15 June 2007, http://www.ethicsdaily.com/article_detail.cfm?AID=9062 (accessed 12 December 2007).

[2] Unless otherwise noted, all Scripture quotations are taken from the New Living Translation (Carol Stream IL: Tyndale House Publishing, 2004).

[3] Genesis 29:32.

[4] Genesis 29:33.

[5] Genesis 29:34.

[6] Genesis 30:6.

[7] Genesis 30:8.

[8] Genesis 30:11.

[9] Genesis 30:13.

[10] Rachel named her final son Ben-Oni, "son of my trouble," giving testimony to the death he brought her, but after her death Jacob changed his name to Benjamin, "son of my right hand." See Genesis 35:18.

[11] *Joseph and the Amazing Technicolor Dreamcoat* is the theatrical work of Andrew Lloyd Webber based on the life of Joseph. The play has been in production since 1968.

[12] Natasha Korecki, "Authorities Say Radio Caller Admitted Heist," *Chicago Sun Times,* 23 February 2005, 6.

[13] "World's largest cut sapphire goes on display after 18 years under discoverer's bed," *Atlanta Journal Constitution,* 12 April 1987, A-46.

[14] "Madeover Ken Hopes to Win Barbie Back," Reuters news release, 10 February 2006, http://www.cnn.com/2006/US/02/09/ken.barbie.reut/ (accessed 12 December 2007).

Life in the Pits

When we ask our question—"Why is God unfair?"—we are really asking, "Why is God unfair to me?" — Philip Yancey

You may remember her story. It is a retelling of just how far jealousy and envy can take a person. At Alice Johnson Junior High School in Channelview, Texas, two eighth grade honor students were competing for a single spot on the freshman cheerleading squad: Amber Heath and Shanna Harper, Wanda Holloway's daughter.

The competition was intense, as it had been between the two girls for most of their school years. Amber won the final spot on the squad, and when it was clear that Shanna would not make it, Wanda could not take it.

Wanda, who had served as the organist at the local Baptist church, plotted to have Amber's mother killed. Her hope was to cause such a degree of emotional stress that Amber would be unable to hold her place on the cheerleading squad. Shanna would then become Amber's substitute. As disturbing as this was, she would have had Amber murdered as well, but the times being what they were, she could only afford a single assassination.

Holloway secured the services of her former brother-in-law to aid in the acquisition of a hit man. This brother-in-law, wanting to avoid entanglements with law enforcement, promptly turned informant, and a tragedy of even greater proportion was averted. For a pair of diamond earrings, Mrs. Heath would have been murdered so that Shanna might make the freshman squad.

Two trials and two made-for-television movies later, Holloway was sentenced to fifteen years in prison. School principal James Barker said of the incident, "After all, it's the American way. We all want our children to achieve. There is a part of Wanda Holloway in all of us."[1]

There was a lot of Wanda Holloway in Joseph's brothers.

When Joseph was born he took from his siblings something that could never be replaced—their father. It was a crime they could not forgive.

In Genesis 37 the brothers Hebrew are grazing their sheep far from home. This was not unusual. Mature grassland was at a premium, and with a large flock the brothers were forced to range far and wide. Jacob, maybe sensing that his boys were up to no good on their faraway grazing adventure, sent the golden boy Joseph to check up on them: "'Go and see how your brothers and the flocks are getting along,' Jacob said. 'Then come back and bring me a report.' So Jacob sent him on his way, and Joseph traveled to Shechem from their home in the valley of Hebron" (Gen 37:14).

Joseph began the tattling journey that would take him to his brothers, to enslavement, to a foreign country, and to his destiny. He hadn't even packed his lunch. On his way he got lost, but came across a stranger who pointed him in the right, or wrong, direction:

> When he arrived there, a man from the area noticed him wandering around the countryside. "What are you looking for?" he asked.
>
> "I'm looking for my brothers," Joseph replied. "Do you know where they are pasturing their sheep?"
>
> "Yes," the man told him. "They have moved on from here, but I heard them say, 'Let's go on to Dothan.'" So Joseph followed his brothers to Dothan and found them there. (Gen 37:15-18)

I admit that I often speculate when reading the Bible. I can't help myself, and I imagine you can't either. This is a good place to do just that. What if this stranger had not crossed paths with Joseph? What if this stranger had not overheard that fateful conversation about the location of Joseph's brothers? What if this stranger had not taken the initiative to ask Joseph what he was looking for? What if, in frustration at not finding his brothers, Joseph had simply returned home?

Surely his father would have forgiven his favorite son of such a failure. Instead, this unknown, unnamed traveler enters and leaves the biblical text with no more than two dozen words. That brief conversation changed the life of a nation.

This is how God works—in the small things, in happenstance, in the could-bes and the might-have-beens. Subtly, in the routine and insignificant,

God steers our lives on their intended paths, mostly without us recognizing it.

Two jobs are offered, you take the one in Omaha rather than St. Louis, and things change forever. Torn between majors, you choose engineering over accounting, and your life's path is set. Badgered into going on a blind date, you finally relent, and twelve years, a mortgage, and three children later, you reflect on just how significant that one decision was.

Sure, Providence of some kind is involved. We just don't always recognize it as such. Sister Virginia Cotter of the Daughters of Charity may say it best: "The mystery of life is not that God is so far away that he cannot be seen, but that he is so close, he is often overlooked."[2]

God's hand, even in the giving of travel directions by a stranger, should not be missed.

Joseph's brothers saw him coming in the distance. How could they miss him, with that colorful coat burning their retinas in the midday sun? The angry resentment seized them anew and they immediately hatched a plan to do away with this conceited prima donna once and for all:

> When Joseph's brothers saw him coming, they recognized him in the distance. As he approached, they made plans to kill him. "Here comes the dreamer!" they said. "Come on, let's kill him and throw him into one of these cisterns. We can tell our father, 'A wild animal has eaten him.' Then we'll see what becomes of his dreams!"
>
> But when Reuben heard of their scheme, he came to Joseph's rescue. "Let's not kill him," he said. "Why should we shed any blood? Let's just throw him into this empty cistern here in the wilderness. Then he'll die without our laying a hand on him." Reuben was secretly planning to rescue Joseph and return him to his father.
>
> So when Joseph arrived, his brothers ripped off the beautiful robe he was wearing. Then they grabbed him and threw him into the cistern. Now the cistern was empty; there was no water in it. (Gen 37:18-24)

Have you ever walked into a room and realized that you were being talked about? It is a strange, cold feeling. What would it be like to walk into a room where your murder was being plotted?

The plot, however, was not unanimous. Reuben, the oldest, showed restraint. He wished maybe to teach the boy a lesson but wanted no harm to come to him. He planned a covert rescue mission that would return Joseph safely to Jacob. Again, in the strange twists and turns of Providence, it was not to be:

> Then, just as they were sitting down to eat, they looked up and saw a caravan of camels in the distance coming toward them. It was a group of Ishmaelite traders taking a load of gum, balm, and aromatic resin from Gilead down to Egypt.
>
> Judah said to his brothers, "What will we gain by killing our brother? His blood would just give us a guilty conscience. Instead of hurting him, let's sell him to those Ishmaelite traders. After all, he is our brother—our own flesh and blood!" And his brothers agreed. So when the Ishmaelites, who were Midianite traders, came by, Joseph's brothers pulled him out of the cistern and sold him to them for twenty pieces of silver. And the traders took him to Egypt.
>
> Some time later, Reuben returned to get Joseph out of the cistern. When he discovered that Joseph was missing, he tore his clothes in grief. Then he went back to his brothers and lamented, "The boy is gone! What will I do now?" (Gen 37:25-30)

At last Joseph's brothers showed a flash of compassion. Judah, suddenly benevolent in mercy, asked, "Why should we kill him? After all, he is our brother!" Instead, Judah decided they would profit from his disappearance.

To avoid an overly guilty conscience, the true motive for their mercy, the brothers sold Joseph as a slave to a rolling flea market long before Rueben was able to intervene. Joseph was carried away as a prisoner, separated from his loving father at the time most teenagers today are just learning to drive.

Again, speculation overtakes me. Where was Rueben? Why had he been delayed in his rescue attempt? Did he not see the arrival of the Ishmaelites? Had he been sitting at lunch with his brothers, the story of Joseph would have been very different.

I have a small inkling of how Joseph felt in that pit. When I was young my uncle owned a chicken farm. This was no barnyard collection of birds. His farm consisted of three huge poultry houses filled with thousands of chickens each. I spent my most formative summers on that farm with him, my aunt, and my grandmother. In the days before improved environmental controls, the birds that died before making it to the processing plant and the supermarket were disposed of in a "chicken pit."

These were poultry landfills. They were constructed by first digging a large hole with machinery. A wooden roof was placed across the top and dead chickens were dropped through a hatch into the pit. Over time the wooden roof would inevitably rot, and before my uncle could replace the broken areas there were nauseating glimpses into the world of some very unlucky birds (if those chicks making it to the processing plant could be considered lucky).

The chicken pit was a sickening, wretched place that words cannot describe. Older cousins—who shall remain nameless—would dangle me by my ankles over this Dante-like abyss, cackling with laughter the entire time. I never thought they wanted to kill me, but I often wondered what would have happened had their sweaty grip failed in the hot Georgia sun. I also wondered, like Joseph probably did, how they could do such a horrible thing to someone who shared their family name.

As the brothers heartlessly sat down to eat their lunch, Joseph cried alone in an empty cistern, a pit. But Joseph would not be the only one who suffered. The brothers committed this terrible offense and returned home, covering their tracks along the way, with a devastating falsehood for their father.

> Then the brothers killed a young goat and dipped Joseph's robe in its blood. They sent the beautiful robe to their father with this message: "Look at what we found. Doesn't this robe belong to your son?"
>
> Their father recognized it immediately. "Yes," he said, "it is my son's robe. A wild animal must have eaten him. Joseph has clearly been torn to pieces!" Then Jacob tore his clothes and dressed himself in burlap. He mourned deeply for his son for a long time. His family all tried to comfort him, but he refused to be comforted. "I will go to my grave mourning for my son," he would say, and then he would weep. (Gen 37:31-35)

So devastating was the news of Joseph's disappearance and probable death that it was almost enough to kill Jacob, and decades later he was still grieving. His sons, unable to confess their transgression and unwilling even to call Joseph "our brother"—rather "your son"—inflicted further cruelty on their aged father. Jacob had to live with the guilt, false though it was, that he had sent his beloved Joseph on the errand that ended his life. It is a cruelty that is almost incomprehensible.

How could children do this to their own father? What darkness would motivate a son to inflict this kind of pain on his aging father?

It was the same darkness that sold Joseph into slavery. It was the darkness of jealousy and resentment. They were repaying Jacob for the favoritism he had shown to Joseph. They rid themselves of the brother they hated, and now punished the father who had created the situation in the first place. Years of living with distrust and envy made revenge much easier than we might imagine. Now Jacob had to live, as well as he could, with the outcome.

How many Jacobs are there—those who drown their pillow every night with sorrowful tears because of the injustice that has found a home under their roof? Those who grieve for years because of the decisions they have made that badly hurt a loved one and can never be reversed? Those who, in confusion, wonder where God is in the anarchy and pain of their lives? Those who must live with the cruelty of others?

My wife Cindy and I recently visited with a young mother enduring a Jacob-like tragedy. This young lady, whom I'll call Tammy, was doing her best to rear two beautiful daughters on her own. She made ends meet by working at an outlet store on weekdays and bartending on weekends. She told us, "I moved here, so far away from home, to escape my psycho family." That well-crafted escape was not successful for long.

Tammy's younger sister, strung out on alcohol and drugs, had been killed in an automobile accident. The sister's four young children, the oldest seven years old, were taken in by Tammy's mother. Tammy's mother then died suddenly during a routine surgical procedure. The four orphans and Tammy's younger, rebellious brother of fourteen all came to live with her. They had no other place to go.

On the evening Cindy and I sat with her and heard her story, between all the kids' shouting and playing, she was exhausted, financially used up, and in a state of near collapse. Tammy had that faraway look in her eyes, the look of someone living in perpetual disbelief.

She finally said, "I think God has a plan in all of this." Turning to me, she asked, "He does, doesn't he?"

I knew why she asked me such a question. I am the minister. I am supposed to have answers to these kinds of questions. She needed reassurance from some kind of "authority" on the subject. But given her situation, I felt it would be an insult to give a pat answer to such a complicated question. I could only give her a weak smile, very weak, and admit that while I believed God had a plan, I had no idea what it was.

I cannot solve the problem of injustice in the world. Most times I cannot even understand it. Who can? But I have learned that "life" and "God" are not always the same thing and should not be confused with each other. Sometimes life is rewarding and makes sense. We should be grateful. Sometimes life is confusing and puzzling. We should be prayerful. And sometimes life is overwhelmingly harsh and unjust. We have little recourse in such cases but to be patient and trusting.

These words will be rejected by some who see every act—good, bad, or ugly—as sourced in the person of God, but maybe that perspective is incomplete. Instead of God being *over* all things in a mechanical, controlling sense where God has an unalterable "plan" for everything, maybe God is *in* all things, taking what life deals and joining his children in their sufferings. Ultimately he brings glory to himself as he weaves our lives with the threads of triumph and tragedy.

In other words, it may help us to understand that it was not God who directly sold Joseph into Egypt, but it was God who went with Joseph into Egypt. It was not God who caused Jacob's heart to break, but it was God who wept with Jacob as he heard that wretched news, and it was God who cried with him every night thereafter. It was not God who took Tammy's sister and mother and then flooded her home with more children than she could possibly care for, but it is God who will be with her every step of the way, providing the grace she needs for a life that is simply unfair.

That God is with us—identifying with our pain, partnering with us in our sorrow, and understanding our sufferings—is the only conclusion to which I can come. As a Christian, and one who believes that the appearance of Jesus is God's greatest identification with our life experiences, I have no other answer to life's injustices than God is with us.

When the angel announced the miraculous birth of the Christ, that exact prophetic name was used: "Immanuel," meaning "God with us." The accusation that God is absent from his creation can no longer make grade. God is not a dementia-struck, teetering old man wandering the hallways of heaven who has lost control of his capacities and his world.

He is in that world, celebrating our victories, enduring our hardships, and bearing our hurts. God may not always rescue us, but he always identifies with us and can never abandon us. We are not alone.

The writer of Hebrews used these words: "Since [Jesus] himself has gone through suffering and testing, he is able to help us when we are being tested" (Heb 2:18). And again:

> So then, since we have a great High Priest who has entered heaven, Jesus the Son of God, let us hold firmly to what we believe. This High Priest of

ours understands our weaknesses, for he faced all of the same testings we
do, yet he did not sin. So let us come boldly to the throne of our gracious
God. There we will receive his mercy, and we will find grace to help us
when we need it most. (Heb 4:14-16)

When tears burn our faces and our hearts break into so many pieces we
think we will never be put together again, we are forced to wrestle with this
God whom we have been told is in complete control of our lives. Granted,
most of us don't stop believing in him, but we do wish we knew what in
heaven or hell he was doing. Where is God now? Why doesn't he intervene?
Why is he ignoring me?

But God is in the pain. God has intervened. He refuses to ignore us. For
he knows what it is like to be found in the fashion of a man and subject himself to suffering, even suffering on a cross. God damned himself to a bloody
execution, not for some theological principle or a faraway heaven, but for
you. For you.

Every time you suffer, you will find him there again. In your most bitter
prayers and violent outbursts against heaven, Christ kneels beside you.
When you cry, Jesus weeps with you. When confusion overwhelms and frus-
trates you, the Lord himself holds your hand and keeps you company. When
you turn your head on the cross of suffering, you will see that it is the
Galilean Rabbi who bleeds and suffers beside you.

I don't know why God allows/permits/causes/tolerates the things that
happen in this world and in our lives. I have given up on that question altogether. I just know that he goes with us through it all.

Dorothy Sayers put it this way: "Whatever reason God chose to make
man as he is—limited and suffering and subject to sorrows and death—he
had the honesty and the courage to take his own medicine. When he was a
man, he played the man. He was born in poverty and died in disgrace and
thought it well worthwhile."[3]

For now, that will have to be enough.

Questions for Reflection

1. Principal James Barker said of the incident involving Shanna Harper and Wanda Holloway, "After all, it's the American way. We all want our children to achieve. There is a part of Wanda Holloway in all of us." Do you believe this is true?

2. Is it always possible to recognize God's specific activity in your life? Give an example of a time when you identified God's work in your life only after the fact.

3. It appears that Joseph's brother Reuben wanted to save Joseph's life. Why was he the only one to defend Joseph? Do you think all the other brothers felt as much hatred toward Joseph as Judah did?

4. Jacob was crushed by the deceit of his sons. Why is it so easy for some to deceive, disregard, or hurt those closest to them (such as parents, siblings, or a spouse)?

5. Tammy finally said to my wife and me, "I think God has a plan in all of this." Then she turned to me and asked, "He does, doesn't he?" How fixed or exact is God's plan for our future? How much of this plan depends upon our actions and decisions?

6. I divide the injustice of "life" from the goodness of "God." Is this a false separation? If so, how do you reconcile or bring the two back together?

Notes

[1] Nancy Gibbs, "Murders They Wrote," *Time* 137/13 (1 April 1991), archived at http://www.time.com/time/magazine/article/0,9171,972639,00.html (accessed 18 December 2007).

[2] Sister Virginia Cotter, lecture, Heritage Speaker Series, Sacred Heart Hospital on the Emerald Coast, Miramar Beach FL, 27 June 2006.

[3] Dorothy Sayers, *Creed or Chaos* (New York: Harcourt Brace, 1949), 4.

Hell Hath No Fury

Well, what am I supposed to do? You won't answer my calls, you change your number. I mean, I'm not gonna be ignored. — Glenn Close in Fatal Attraction

When Joseph was taken to Egypt by the Ishmaelite traders, he was purchased by Potiphar, an Egyptian officer. Potiphar was captain of the guard for Pharaoh, the king of Egypt. — Genesis 39:1

In the space of a few verses, a few days, Joseph has gone from being the princely son of his enormous family to being a slave in a faraway land—a land that generations earlier had brought near destruction to his great-grandfather, Abraham.

Abraham had ventured into Egypt to save his fledgling family from starvation. Before it was over, he had experienced the ancient equivalent of being tarred, feathered, and run out of the country on a rail, fortunate to escape with his life.

There is little doubt that when the family gathered around their evening fire to eat dinner, Joseph heard the horror stories of the past. Egypt was that strange place of strange people so unlike the Hebrew shepherds and of multiple strange gods so different from Yahweh.

Rising from the African sand, Egypt held nothing but trouble for the children of Abraham. It was to be avoided at all costs. I imagine Egypt had become that mythical place used by Hebrew parents to keep their rebellious little boys in line: "Be a good boy or you'll end up in Egypt."

Now Joseph was a prisoner there.

Steven Linscott was born in Newport, Rhode Island, the son of a career Navy man. Over the course of his childhood he lived in a half-dozen flotilla towns before the family settled in Ellsworth, Maine. Steven enjoyed a pleasant enough youth and entered college in the early 1970s with the characteristics of most college-bound young people: searching, questioning, and more than a little confused over the meaning of life.

He ultimately decided to follow in his father's footsteps and join the Navy. It was a good decision. Steven excelled, winning accolades from his peers and commanding officers. While outwardly he was nothing but successful, internally he remained confused and conflicted, particularly in regard to issues of faith. Christianity had roused his curiosity, but with mounting philosophical questions and few answers, he was on the verge of dismissing the faith without further consideration.

Early on the morning before Thanksgiving 1974, Steven went to the naval base coffee shop to wrestle further with his questions. On the previous night he had poured out his spiritual frustration on paper. Reviewing his notes and rising early, he was determined to settle his mind.

A fellow sailor, a man he had never met, was in the coffee shop that morning. The two struck up a conversation, and in an unplanned turn of fortune this stranger shared the Christian faith with Steven. It was the beginning of a conversion.

After years of searching for meaning and truth, Steven came running to Christ with abandon. He finished his tour of duty, married Ms. Lois Beverly, the daughter of Christian missionaries, and moved to Oak Park, Illinois, to attend Emmaus Bible College. Steven and Lois committed themselves and their young family to the ministry of serving Christ and serving others.[1]

Joseph had to be thinking as he was drug through the sand to Egypt, "This is the worst thing that has ever happened to me." He was right. It was the worst thing ever to happen to him. But it was the best worst thing ever to happen.

He could have been lying at the bottom of an empty cistern, his life ebbing away. He could have become the property of the caravan owner to whom he was first sold, sentenced to the wandering existence of some kind of gypsy. He could have been purchased on the slave market by a cruel taskmaster and wound up cutting stone in the Egyptian desert for what would have certainly been a short, miserable life.

Instead Joseph became the property of Potiphar, a high-ranking governmental official. With this turn of coincidental Providence, he was on his way to the pinnacle of world power—a place where his dreams would come true.

Divine intervention, Providence, fate, destiny: Pick the word you think fits best. It oozes from the pages of Joseph's story. In spite of his many difficulties, God's favor seems to follow Joseph wherever he goes. Observe what happens upon his arrival in Potiphar's house:

> The Lord was with Joseph, so he succeeded in everything he did as he served in the home of his Egyptian master. Potiphar noticed this and realized that the Lord was with Joseph, giving him success in everything he did. This pleased Potiphar, so he soon made Joseph his personal attendant. He put him in charge of his entire household and everything he owned. From the day Joseph was put in charge of his master's household and property, the Lord began to bless Potiphar's household for Joseph's sake. All his household affairs ran smoothly, and his crops and livestock flourished. So Potiphar gave Joseph complete administrative responsibility over everything he owned. With Joseph there, he didn't worry about a thing—except what kind of food to eat! (Gen 39:2-6)

The text says the Lord made Joseph successful. The New International Version says Joseph "prospered" in Potiphar's house. Joseph prospered. This is a much-abused word in the Christian universe.

Certain spiritual entrepreneurs would have us believe that God's intention for us all is an expensive car, an early retirement, and a healthy financial portfolio. Wealth, prosperity, financial security—these are the marks of spirituality, and they wait for the taking, for those with enough faith to seize them.

But financial gain is more often the mark of American capitalism than of the Christian faith. Joseph had none of these things. He was a slave. He owned nothing. His prosperity was not measured in material wealth but by an abundance of divine favor.

God had placed his hand upon Joseph in an astonishing way. He was being prepared and fashioned for great things. Even Potiphar, steeped in the ancient polytheism and mysticism of Egypt, recognized this.

What a great lesson for Christ's followers today. Joseph, through hard work, integrity, and a quiet trust in God, had earned the respect—even admiration—of one who was not a follower of his God. This was his success. This was his prosperity.

Some Christians spend a great deal of energy demanding to be heard or demanding that those around them honor their right of speech. These seem to forget that being heard is a right that is earned, not commanded. A well-known verse easily quoted by many, 1 Peter 3:15 reads, "If someone asks about your Christian hope, always be ready to explain it." But the text, apparently unknown to some, continues, "But do this in a gentle and respectful way. Keep your conscience clear. Then if people speak against you, they will be ashamed when they see what a good life you live because you belong to Christ" (vv. 16 and 17).

In the early morning hours of Saturday, October 4, 1980, Steven Linscott awoke horrified by a dreadful nightmare. He had dreamed of a light complexioned, square-built man attacking and killing a young woman. The dream had been frighteningly detailed.

In his underwear and a near-panicked sweat, Steven walked through his Oak Park apartment checking on his young children. Finally, he returned to bed, shaken, but determined to get back to sleep.

Later in the day two policemen stood outside Steven and Lois's door. A neighbor, Karen Ann Phillips, an attractive, energetic twenty-four-year-old nursing student, had been beaten to death during the night.

Two days later Steven decided to contact the police and tell them about his dream. He had mixed emotions. On one hand he felt silly. This seemed so impractical. On the other hand he wanted to do his civic duty. He drafted a seven-paragraph account of the nightmare that had robbed him of sleep the same night Ms. Phillips had been killed. He innocently thought the dream and murder might be connected.

On Tuesday, November 25, 1980, Steven Linscott was arrested and charged with the murder of Karen Ann Phillips. Police and state prosecutors claimed Linscott's recounting of the dream was his way of confessing his guilt, and any discrepancies between the crime and the dream were his way of distancing himself from it. While physical evidence gathered at the scene implicated Steven, it did the same to sixty percent of the male population. Steven Linscott was only one of more than two million males in the greater Chicago area who could have murdered Phillips.

The Linscotts were so overwhelmed by what had happened to them that they rarely considered that Steven would actually be convicted of the crime.

The very thought was unspeakable. A trial would vindicate him. Their conclusion was that God would not allow such a miscarriage of justice to happen to someone so committed to Christ.

That conclusion was misplaced.

On Thursday, May 27, 1982, some eighteen months after his initial arrest, Steven Linscott faced a trial by a jury of his peers. Three weeks later he was found guilty of the murder. Judge Adam Stillo of the Fourth District Circuit Court, with the pathetic words, "Good luck," sentenced Linscott to forty years in prison.

The sentence was devastating. Steven met his incarceration with courage, but also misery. Often reduced to despondency and bitter tears, he feared for his wife and children who would now have to live alone. He peppered heaven with questions: Why has God abandoned me? Does God no longer love or care for me? How could he leave me in a place like this?

Steven knew God wasn't dead, but was convinced that he was, in fact, deaf. Apparently, God intentionally wanted to be a disappointment.[2]

Joseph, an insignificant Hebrew slave, had earned the privilege of respect and trust from the very one who owned him. Life was improving. Things were looking up. Joseph was advancing. But Joseph was not the only one on the move. Potiphar's wife was making advancements of her own.

> Joseph was a very handsome and well-built young man, and Potiphar's wife soon began to look at him lustfully. "Come and sleep with me," she demanded. But Joseph refused. "Look," he told her, "my master trusts me with everything in his entire household. No one here has more authority than I do. He has held back nothing from me except you, because you are his wife. How could I do such a wicked thing? It would be a great sin against God."
>
> She kept putting pressure on Joseph day after day, but he refused to sleep with her, and he kept out of her way as much as possible. (Gen 39:6-10)

I usually snub the trite little sayings on church signs, but one I saw recently could serve as a summary of these verses: "Opportunity may knock once, but temptation bangs on the door all day long."

Relentlessly this woman pursued Joseph. And why not? She was accustomed to having anything and everything she desired. Her husband was a wealthy, powerful man commanding enough prestige to have a house full of servants. She lived at the upper reaches of Egyptian society, and if Potiphar was too busy and she too bored, why not pass the time with this handsome new edition to the house staff?

Joseph, while confined to the life of a servant, would not play the role of her sex slave. He rebuffed her advances time and time again, clinging fiercely to his integrity. Finally, she would have no more of his refusals.

> One day, however, no one else was around when he went in to do his work. She came and grabbed him by his cloak, demanding, "Come on, sleep with me!" Joseph tore himself away, but he left his cloak in her hand as he ran from the house.
>
> When she saw that she was holding his cloak and he had fled, she called out to her servants. Soon all the men came running. "Look!" she said. "My husband has brought this Hebrew slave here to make fools of us! He came into my room to rape me, but I screamed. When he heard me scream, he ran outside and got away, but he left his cloak behind with me."
>
> She kept the cloak with her until her husband came home. Then she told him her story. "That Hebrew slave you've brought into our house tried to come in and fool around with me," she said. "But when I screamed, he ran outside, leaving his cloak with me!"
>
> Potiphar was furious when he heard his wife's story about how Joseph had treated her. So he took Joseph and threw him into the prison where the king's prisoners were held, and there he remained. (Gen 39:11-20)

Joseph couldn't seem to keep his shirt on. Once, his top coat was used to falsify his death. This time, it was used to frame Joseph for an attempted rape. Slanderously and slyly, Potiphar's wife derided the former object of her passion with the racial jab "that Hebrew." In her vengeance she used false accusations to scuttle whatever future Joseph had. Potiphar returned home angry and was forced to take action.

Why was Potiphar so angry? The text never states that his anger was directed at Joseph. Indeed, I do not believe Joseph was the object of his wrath. Potiphar was angry over the situation in which he had been placed. He was angry with a wife who had masterfully manipulated the entire household. Yes, Potiphar threw Joseph into prison, but what other choice did he have?

Had Potiphar truly believed the accusation, he could and would certainly have executed Joseph on the spot. He had the power to do so. Why would Potiphar allow a man whom he had trusted with his whole household live after taking advantage of that trust? And why place him in a "white collar" prison where only political prisoners were kept? The prison that would become Joseph's home was no Alcatraz.

Maybe it was because Potiphar knew all too well the kind of woman he was living with—an unprincipled trollop not accustomed to taking "no" for an answer. The only way for Potiphar to keep peace at home and save face with his entire staff, a staff that now knew the accusation against Joseph well, was to punish the offender in some way, even though Potiphar had to know Joseph was innocent.

Over the course of his imprisonment, Steven Linscott's faith returned and strengthened. He threw himself on the mercies of God to sustain him, and contrary to earlier conclusions, God did not disappoint. Steven gathered his composure enough to continue his college studies, obtain his degree, and eventually become an award-winning editor of *The Forum*, the prison's newspaper.

Meanwhile, hundreds of supporters kept their pressure on Illinois authorities to review the Linscott conviction. Steven's wife and children were cared for by those who had heard about the case from all over the United States. Their legal bills were underwritten by several Christian businessmen who had become convinced of Steven's innocence. *Christianity Today* ran an article titled "The Strange Case of Steven Linscott," and readers of that publication were alarmed at the inequality so evident in the judicial system.[3]

Public opinion was galvanized by the events of Steven's case. After all, there had never been a confession of guilt. There was no eyewitness testimony. No fingerprints were found at the murder scene. No specific physical evidence linking Steven directly to the crime had ever been collected or presented. There was no proof that Steven had even met Karen Ann Phillips. Still, he sat in state prison because of his inexplicable dream.

In December 1983, the Linscott case returned to the courtroom on appeal. His defense team performed brilliantly and passionately, focusing years of frustration into those critical moments before the appellate court. The court considered the Linscott case for eighteen additional months before making a ruling. Finally, in a split decision, the court reversed the conviction on grounds that guilt had not been proven beyond a reasonable doubt. Steven would be released!

Just hours before his release, however, Steven was returned to his cell when the state appealed to the Illinois Supreme Court. Justice Daniel P.

Ward issued an emergency order halting Linscott's release until the entire Supreme Court could hear the case. Two years later—two years!—the Supreme Court released Steven on bail, pending the final outcome of their ruling.

A year later, the same court astonishingly reversed their decision and reinstated the original conviction. Steven Linscott returned to prison.

Joseph's dreams of destiny and power were exactly that as he took up residence behind bars—dreams. He had performed well, acted justly, and maintained his integrity. Where had it gotten him? Thrown in prison.

Everyone suffers, but to do the right thing only to be punished for it, to act with truthfulness only to pay the price, is a most bitter pill to swallow. It's easy to moralize about honesty being the best policy, but "honesty is not the only policy."[4] The world is overrun with those who have filled their coffers by deceptive means, by those who have scraped and scratched their way to the top of the hill without conscience. They, not unlike Joseph's brothers and Potiphar's wife, seem to sleep well enough even though they have ruined the lives and futures of the innocent.

Such villains seem never to suffer or pay for their crimes. How does one maintain faith in times of such gross injustice? The Scriptures do not tell us exactly how Joseph did it, but somehow he did. A clue may come from the Hebrew Psalms.

There are more than a hundred psalms in the Old Testament, one for every occasion it seems. Many of these are psalms of lament, psalms of complaint in which the writer begs for divine intervention, for an injustice to be corrected, or for the God-given strength to persevere.

Some of these laments are corporate—the entire community is crying out to God. Others are individual and personal. The psalmist is alone, abandoned, and forgotten, not unlike Joseph.

Lament psalms have been a great help to me, but they are not my favorite passages of Scripture for a couple of reasons. First, these psalms almost always hover around the subject of patience, of waiting on God. That's not something I enjoy, nor am I very good at it. Second, it seems that every time I settle on an Old Testament lament, I'm in some kind of trouble.

I'm drawn to these passages in times of pain, I suppose, seeking a writer who understands my feelings. But I'm also drawn to these passages for the encouragement. The language of lament is powerful in its expression of genuine faith, for the truest evidence of faith is the willingness to wait on God.

At no time are our doubts more intense than when God makes us wait. Generally, we don't sit around and wonder, "Is there a God out there somewhere?" Christians have settled this question. Instead, we flounder about in our prayer closets and wonder why he behaves the way he does.

If God is out there—this all-powerful, all-loving God—and if I am his child, should he not be concerned about this mess I'm in? Does he care that my life is in ruins, that my heart is broken? Will he not rally to save me, to deliver me?

These are the questions raised in the dark night of the soul. These are the questions with which the psalmists grappled. With the language of lament, the biblical writers capture our own thoughts and frustrations; there are few believers who have not been confused over the actions, timing, or absence of the Almighty.

This confusion sometimes crosses over into rage. As an example, hear a portion of Psalm 109, written by none other than David himself. Speaking of his enemies, he cried out in prayer to God:

> Let his years be few;
>   let someone else take his position.
> May his children become fatherless,
>   and his wife a widow.
>   May his children wander as beggars
>   and be driven from their ruined homes.
> May creditors seize his entire estate,
>   and strangers take all he has earned.
> Let no one be kind to him;
>   let no one pity his fatherless children.
> May all his offspring die.
> May his family name be blotted out in a single generation.
> May the Lord never forget the sins of his fathers;
>   may his mother's sins never be erased from the record.
> May the Lord always remember these sins,
>   and may his name disappear from human memory.

Or consider Psalm 137:8-9:

> Happy is the one who pays you back for what
>   you have done to us.
> Happy is the one who takes your babies and
>   smashes them against the rocks!

How did this stuff get in the Bible? How could God allow this kind of talk to make it into the Scriptures? This talk about destroying people, humiliating them, praying that babies would have their brains bashed out? This doesn't sound very Christian, does it?

Before you cast judgment too quickly, ask yourself one question: have you ever thought or felt similar things as the psalmists write? The raw, honest passion that flows from the psalmists' pens is the raw, honest passion flowing from the human heart.

We are given the privilege to look over the writers' shoulders, as it were, as they write, converse, and argue with God. The question is not, "How could God allow this stuff to get into the Bible?" The better question is, "How could God not allow such things to be recorded in the Bible?" For it is honest. It is real. It is what life and faith are really like.

These Old Testament writers were close enough to God to unload on him. They were close enough to let their feelings, wishes, even their dreams of revenge all hang out. God knew these things already. These writers had the integrity to admit it.

I have two or three friends to whom I can say almost anything. Hopefully, you have the same. These friends will hear my words and, like eating chicken, will swallow the meat and spit out the bones. If I am angry, lonely, frustrated, elated, celebrative, it doesn't matter—they listen. They understand. They allow me to give full expression to how I feel. They can take it, without my words or emotions endangering our friendship.

God can take it too. When I heave up my fiercest anger and deepest resentments to and at God, I do so precisely because I trust him. I believe, with whatever faith I have left, that he can stomach my disappointment. I discover that God is generous enough to field my accusations and disgust without abandoning me. Strangely, the questions and finger pointing railed against heaven are a form of faith.

In 1992, with the emergence of DNA testing, Steven Linscott was finally exonerated for the murder of Karen Ann Phillips. Genetic tests failed to link Linscott to the crime. After more than a decade of imprisonment, all charges were dropped and he was set free. Ten years later, in 2002, Steve received a gubernatorial pardon, expulsing his entire record.

He and his wife, Lois, who never wavered in her commitment to her husband over thirty years of marriage, now live in Springfield, Illinois, where Steven is a counselor for abused and emotionally disturbed children.

Following his ordeal Linscott said,

My lawyer and I found there were fifty-seven major differences between my dream and the murder . . . but the police said my hairs were found at the scene. It was my two-year-old daughter's hair they used to match. They said my blood was at the scene, but the evidence was fabricated and an appeals court said it was prosecutorial misconduct.[5]

It is Lois who may sum up their perspective best:

I was very angry at God. Everything in me wanted to throw in the towel. I was tired of praying . . . trying to get on God's good side. But . . . [I remembered] the response of Peter to the Lord when he asked His disciples, "Will you also go away?"

A lot of folks had left Him. Peter said, "Well, where else shall we go? There's no alternative. You're the best choice we got." That's the only thing I could think of—I don't have any alternatives. The alternative was anger and bitterness and the desire for revenge. The Lord rewarded me for just hanging on.[6]

Karen Ann Phillips's murder has never been solved.

Questions for Reflection

1. Put yourself in Joseph's place as he arrived in Egypt. What feelings would you have had toward your brothers? Toward Potiphar? Toward God?

2. Have you ever experienced a "best worst thing" when what first appeared as a personal disaster led to something beautiful?

3. I propose that Joseph's prosperity in Potiphar's house was not related to material wealth. Does God want his children to be wealthy? How much of our affluence as Americans shades our understanding of the Bible?

4. When it came to the accusation of rape, did Potiphar believe his wife or Joseph? Why?

5. The Steven Linscott case is an incredible example of injustice. What would it have been like to be Steven in prison, though innocent of any crime? Can you imagine what it would have been like to be his spouse? Why would God allow this kind of injustice to take place?

6. Have you ever been instructed never to question God? Is it a lack of faith to question God's actions? Explain.

Notes

[1] Gordon Haresign, *Innocence: The True Story of Steve Linscott* (Grand Rapids: Zondervan, 1986).

[2] Ibid.

[3] Randy Frame, "The Strange Case of Steven Linscott," *Christianity Today* 27 (4 February 1983): 42-44.

[4] Frederick Buechner, *The Magnificent Defeat* (New York: HarperSanFrancisco, 1985), 15.

[5] *Chicago Tribune*, 20 December 2002.

[6] Ibid.

From the Outhouse to the Penthouse

I can't climb from this valley, there's no way I can; I can't do much of nothin', but with God's help I can. — *Bill Evett*

Artie Whitfield Bearden, my maternal grandmother, was a woman like no other I have known. For the thirty-two years she was a part of my life, she lived in a small house at the edge of my uncle's farm. She owned very little—a smattering of furniture, her clothing, a few gardening tools.

When she died there was less than five hundred dollars in her checking account, and nearly a century of living did not fill up her two-bedroom home. Still, that century of living could not be contained in her seven children and nineteen grandchildren.

Some of my most vivid memories of her are focused around her kitchen. It was a Southern paradise: apple and chocolate pies, homemade biscuits, red velvet cake, sawmill gravy, fried chicken in an old iron skillet. On any given day, any or all of these could be found on her table. But there was a lot more to this woman than her culinary skills.

She had a quiet resolve and a peace and strength about life and circumstances that seemed to transcend her surroundings. Though I did not always know it at the time, conversations and interactions in that kitchen were instructional courses in endurance.

A freshman history professor once assigned my class the task of interviewing someone who had lived through the Great Depression or World War II. Grandmother, as everyone called her, was the obvious choice. I sat with her for the better part of an afternoon. Armed with paper, pencil, and a tape recorder, I asked questions and took notes.

She had been born one generation removed from the Civil War. Her mother had died when she was barely weaned, and an older sister had become surrogate mother for the family.

As a child and as a teenager she heard the stories of the Great War, and a few of the farm boys she knew even went away to Europe to fight the Germans. She married my farmer grandfather at the height of America's economic collapse, but she had no historical appreciation for the Depression. In her words, "Somebody said there was one, a depression, I mean. But I don't know about that. All I know is that it was bad before the thirties and bad after that, too."

She gave birth to eight children, and only one, my mother, was born in a hospital. Electricity and indoor plumbing were luxuries that didn't arrive to her sharecropping home until the country, including one of her sons, was involved in a war with a small Asian country called Vietnam.

In the course of her lifetime, she witnessed the advent of nuclear power, space travel, the television, air conditioning, disposable diapers, crossword puzzles, the radio, penicillin, Tupperware, bubble gum, the microwave oven, McDonalds, cellular phones, 8-tracks, and MP3s. The changes imposed upon her otherwise plain life boggle the mind.

Through it all she was married to a man who could only be described as wretched. Floyd Bearden was plagued by the demons of depression, addiction, and alcoholism. He was given to violence, public drunkenness, and squalor. She was victimized by his abuse and wayward ways for decades. But for a Southern woman living in the middle of the twentieth century with seven children on a sharecropper cotton farm, escaping such a marriage was impossible. It might as well have been a prison. While she refused to speak ill of my grandfather, she often intimated that it was only after his death that she experienced the most peaceful days of her adult life.

My interview with her on a cool October afternoon was a high-water mark for me. For the first time I grasped the true mettle of this woman. Sure, I had eaten at her table more times than my own. I had spent every summer in her house. I had listened to her stories and heeded her instructions. I loved and admired her more than any other person on the planet. Now I understood why.

She was more than a blood relative or a doting old woman with an eighth grade education. She was heroic and an example to which I could only hope to aspire.

She had survived the death of her mother, Reconstruction, two World Wars, the Depression, poverty, the death of a child, years of primitive living in the Georgia hills, abject abuse and marital exploitation, and the dispersion of her family to faraway places. At the end of the interview I finally asked her, "How did you do it? How did you raise these kids by yourself with no money, no electricity, no disposable diapers, and with the world against you?"

She stared out the window of her living room for a while. It seemed as if she were consulting with the massive oak tree in the front yard, the only thing on the property older than her. Finally, she chuckled and her round stomach shook beneath her worn dress. With the light of mischief still alive in her dark brown eyes, she said, "I just did what I could. God Almighty took care of the rest."

At some thirty years of age, Joseph was in prison far from the comforts of home. He and his youth were wasting away for a crime he did not commit. He had been victimized by enough injustice to fill ten lifetimes. Still, he was doing what he could.

As he did in Potiphar's house, in prison he rose once again to a place of responsibility, becoming the chief trustee, administrator over the prison. This position was more than a reward for good behavior or an occupation acquired through skillful administration. This was a preparation course for greatness.

Unknown to Joseph, the demands of saving an entire country would soon bear down on him. The lives and futures of millions would be placed in his hands. This prison was a classroom. Graduation and job placement were just over the horizon.

During this time, two high-level prisoners came under Joseph's supervision: Pharaoh's cup-bearer and chief baker, the men most responsible for the ruler of the land's food service. The two were deeply troubled, not only over their imprisonment, but because bad dreams had robbed them of sleep.

Our friend Joseph knew a few things about dreams. He gave them a hearing and offered, with God's help, an interpretation.

So the chief cup-bearer told Joseph his dream first. "In my dream," he said, "I saw a grapevine in front of me. The vine had three branches that began to bud and blossom, and soon it produced clusters of ripe grapes. I was holding Pharaoh's wine cup in my hand, so I took a cluster of grapes and squeezed the juice into the cup. Then I placed the cup in Pharaoh's hand."

"This is what the dream means," Joseph said. "The three branches represent three days. Within three days Pharaoh will lift you up and restore you to your position as his chief cup-bearer. And please remember me and do me a favor when things go well for you. Mention me to Pharaoh, so he might let me out of this place. For I was kidnapped from my homeland, the land of the Hebrews, and now I'm here in prison, but I did nothing to deserve it."

When the chief baker saw that Joseph had given the first dream such a positive interpretation, he said to Joseph, "I had a dream, too. In my dream there were three baskets of white pastries stacked on my head. The top basket contained all kinds of pastries for Pharaoh, but the birds came and ate them from the basket on my head."

"This is what the dream means," Joseph told him. "The three baskets also represent three days. Three days from now Pharaoh will lift you up and impale your body on a pole. Then birds will come and peck away at your flesh." (Gen 40:9-19)

Cloak-and-dagger assassination attempts were not uncommon in ancient times. A king or sultan would surround himself only with those he explicitly trusted. Nowhere was this more necessary than in relation to those who screened and prepared his food. A poisoned glass of wine or a compromised meal would end the reign of the most forceful potentate. Cup-bearers and bakers were on the front lines of defense . . . or conspiracy.

The imprisonment of these two house servants was probably the result of just such a plot against Pharaoh's life. Even with the necessary precautions taken, background checks are not always enough. Someone in the kitchen was likely involved, and the two managers were placed under arrest until guilt or innocence could be confirmed. In the case of the cup-bearer, he was found to be innocent and resumed his normal duties. The baker was condemned to execution, sending an ominous public message to any future would-be conspirators.

The dreams of these men always garner a great deal of attention. That is fair enough. The dreams, and their subsequent interpretations, are remarkable. But I cannot help being more impressed by Joseph's impassioned plea to the cup-bearer: "Mention me to Pharaoh, so he might let me out of this place."

Some commentators see Joseph's request as a lack of trust in God. They reason that Joseph apparently lost faith and took matters into his own hands by attempting to orchestrate his own rescue. I simply cannot follow that line of thinking. Rather, it seems that Joseph seized the opportunity that lay before him. This cup-bearer would once again have the ear of Pharaoh—the highest court in the land. If ever there was a prospect for escaping the injustices of his life, this was it.

Joseph refused to play the role of victim, hopelessly languishing in prison. The fire of life still burned in his belly. Along with his ever-present trust in God was the tenacity to act, to do something, to play his role. Waiting on God is patient work, but it is not idle work. While he waited, Joseph did what he could.

Mount Pinatubo erupted in the Philippines in summer 1991. The volcano had been considered dormant, with no activity since the fourteenth century. When it erupted unexpectedly, more than 200 people were killed and 200,000 were displaced. One people group, the Aetas, were especially devastated by the eruption and the days that followed. The Aeta tribe is a group of aboriginal people who live on the slopes of Mount Pinatubo. For them, Pinatubo is a place of destiny. They have no choice but to call this dangerous mountain home.

After the eruption, the Filipino government planned to build new settlements and permanently relocate the Aetas. These plans were eventually frustrated by the lack of cooperation from the Aetas. Two years after the eruption, the Aetas became tired of waiting in camps and commenced the return to their homes on the volcano's slopes—against the instructions of Western geologists and Filipino authorities.

The Aetas are ruled by doom. They continue to refuse assistance and safe relocation due to mistrustfulness of modern conveniences and the conclusion that a divine fate dictates their future. Pinatubo is not merely a place they call home. It is the only place they feel they can live.[1]

This kind of fatalism once played a prominent role in American life as well. One factor formerly identified in the surprisingly high rate of tornado fatalities in the Southern Bible Belt was the belief that all events are inevitable and people should submit to their fate without protest. Upon hearing a tornado warning, those in the Midwest, Great Plains, and other portions of the country responded with action. They sought shelter, went to the basement, or got out of the path of the storm.

Southerners, steeped in a kind of Christian fatalism, understood the threat as an inescapable act of God. They saw themselves as powerless to act. They huddled in their clapboard houses and prayed for deliverance. This type of fatalism has thankfully eroded due to maturity and education. Those in the South now respond to storm warnings as well as anyone. There was a time when this was not the case at all.[2]

Many of us maintain this same kind of blind fatalism in our personal lives. When the world collapses around us, we resign ourselves to a life of misery, waiting for the other shoe to drop. We give up. This is our fate; our end; the only path destined for us.

Not Joseph. Even in prison, with his actions severely limited, still he acted. He said to the cup-bearer, "Remember me. Take my case to Pharaoh!" Joseph was trusting God, but he was also appealing to the judicial and civil powers. Joseph did what he could do, even when there were no immediate dividends for his actions.

> Pharaoh's birthday came three days later, and he prepared a banquet for all his officials and staff. He summoned his chief cup-bearer and chief baker to join the other officials. He then restored the chief cup-bearer to his former position, so he could again hand Pharaoh his cup. But Pharaoh impaled the chief baker, just as Joseph had predicted when he interpreted his dream. Pharaoh's chief cup-bearer, however, forgot all about Joseph, never giving him another thought.
>   Two full years later . . . . (Gen 40:20–41:1)

Would the ill treatment ever end? Joseph was forgotten for two full years. Two more years of prison duty. Two more years of wasted time. Two more years of paying for the sins of others. Two more years of anger, bitterness, and resentment. Two more years of insult and injustice.

Still, Joseph was resilient. In fact, resiliency separates those who ultimately prevail from those who surrender to their circumstances. It is the stuff of which Joseph was made.

What does resiliency look like? Scores of studies have been conducted in recent years analyzing the survival skills of prisoners of war, victims of prolonged sexual abuse, and other trauma survivors. Resiliency is the ability to bounce back in the face of great difficulty; the knack within a person to bend, but not break, under pressure.

Resiliency enables a person to face the crippling effects of adversity and to overcome. When disaster strikes, those with this kind of endurance adapt, persevere, and somehow even thrive. These hardy souls learn to keep living without the paralysis of fear and panic. Ernest Hemingway wrote, "The world breaks everyone and afterwards many are strong at the broken places."[3] That is resiliency. That is Joseph.

This one who could have resigned himself to victimization became a survivor. It's not that he didn't feel the heat of the pressure cooker. Certainly he did. Doubtless, he grew downhearted and depressed on a regular basis. He simply did not allow these to define his life or his future. Difficult circumstances were instead like a tiller breaking up the soil. They allowed all manner of new life to burst forth and bloom in Joseph's life.

Joseph's stamina finally paid off. Pharoah, the king of Egypt, was also a dreamer. He had baffling dreams of fat and skinny cows rising from the Nile River. In his sleep he saw alternating images of bulging and skeletal heads of grain. Disturbed to the point of panic, he called for all the magicians and wise men of Egypt to interpret his nighttime visions. But no one could help him. It was only then that the chief cup-bearer remembered Joseph:

> "Today I have been reminded of my failure," he told Pharaoh. "Some time ago, you were angry with the chief baker and me, and you imprisoned us in the palace of the captain of the guard. One night the chief baker and I each had a dream, and each dream had its own meaning. There was a young Hebrew man with us in the prison who was a slave of the captain of the guard. We told him our dreams, and he told us what each of our dreams meant. And everything happened just as he had predicted. I was restored to my position as cup-bearer, and the chief baker was executed and impaled on a pole."
>
> Pharaoh sent for Joseph at once, and he was quickly brought from the prison. (Gen 41:1-14)

George Allen became head coach of the Washington Redskins in 1971. With a successful and colorful coaching résumé, he promised the fans that he could fashion the Redskins into champions. He promised them the Super Bowl by the second season, and he delivered. But there was a time when the Redskins seemed far from realizing that destiny. They began to lose badly. Hopes of the postseason seemed to be slithering away. The blame fell not so much on Coach Allen, but on legendary Redskins quarterback Sonny Jurgensen.

Jurgensen played eighteen professional seasons, eleven of those with Washington. He played in five pro bowls, and no less than Vince Lombardi called Jurgensen the greatest pure passer he ever saw play the game. Jurgensen was inducted into the National Football League Hall of Fame in 1983.

For all these accomplishments, Jurgensen's greatest trait was the intangible quality of resiliency. How could a man play nearly twenty NFL seasons with 300-pound defenders trying to decapitate him without it? After an especially disappointing Washington defeat, Sonny was cleaning up in the locker room, getting ready to go home. A reporter snagged the quarterback and asked him if all the criticism and ill treatment made him want to quit.

Jurgensen leaned back, gave a toothless grin, and said, "No, not really. I don't want to quit. I've been in this game long enough to know that every quarterback, every week of the season, spends his time either in the penthouse or in the outhouse."[4]

For more than a dozen years Joseph had been living in the outhouse, forced to eek out a living from the refuse of most everyone who crossed his path. Betrayed. Sold into slavery. Falsely accused and condemned. Imprisoned. Forgotten.

Yet, with a single kingly summons, Joseph left the hell of the last decade and prepared to walk into the palace of world power. It would be the impossible equivalent today of moving from Leavenworth to the Oval Office in the course of an afternoon.

The concierge was holding the elevator for Joseph. His next stop was the penthouse.

Questions for Reflection

1. My grandmother was a powerful example in my life. Has anyone in your life had that kind of influence on you?

2. Joseph asked the cup-bearer to take his case to Pharaoh upon release. Do you think this demonstrated a lack of faith on Joseph's part? Why or why not?

3. "The Aetas continue to refuse assistance and safe relocation due to mistrustfulness of modern conveniences and the conclusion that a divine fate dictates their future." Why do you think the Aetas feel this way? Do you know anyone who feels powerless against divine fate?

4. Joseph displayed true resiliency. Why do some people seem to have this quality while others do not?

5. Pharaoh's cup-bearer forgot Joseph for two full years. Was this a poor memory, God's design, or something else?

6. Have you ever moved from the "outhouse to the penthouse"? Vice versa? What was that like?

Notes

[1] Ilan Kelman, "Role of Technology in Managing Vulnerability to Natural Disasters, with Case Studies of Volcanic Disasters on Non-Industrialized Islands," Master's thesis, Graduate Department of Civil Engineering, University of Toronto, 1998, 87-98.

[2] Matthew D. Biddle and David R. Legates, "Warning Response and Risk Behavior in the Oak Grove-Birmingham, Alabama, Tornado of 08 April 1998," www.colorado.edu/hazards/research (accessed 20 December 2006).

[3] Ernest Hemingway, *A Farewell to Arms* (New York: Scribner Classic Edition, 1997), 249.

[4] Adapted from Charles Swindoll, *Hand Me Another Brick*, rev. ed. (Nashville: W Publishing Group, 1998), 111-12.

The Right Man in the Right Place at the Right Time

*A man is influenced more by what's behind him than what's in front of him;
it is a manifestation of his character when a man can utilize both.*

—Ferrol Sams

Jeff Taylor spent six years at the University of Massachusetts. He never graduated. This did not stop him in 1989 from founding his own successful business: Adion, Incorporated. It was a specialty recruitment and advertising agency.

Five years later, Taylor awoke one morning with a "monster" idea. Putting his ad agency in jeopardy, he started an online meeting place to connect employers and job seekers. There were fewer than 500 commercial websites at the time, and Taylor's site had only a half-dozen clients.

In January 1999, Monster.com, as it is known today, was officially born. The site now boasts more than twelve million visitors a month and has reshaped job hunting for the third millennium. The Monster network shapes and pitches its product—job listings—for the United States, the United Kingdom, Australia, Canada, France, India, and seventeen other countries. The Monster site is, well, monstrous. Job listings, résumé postings, extensive search tools, salary comparisons—you name it. If it pertains to employment, they have it.

A most helpful tab on the site is one titled "Career Advice." There you can find everything from educational opportunities to suggestions for negotiating a higher salary. I found the following tips for surviving the all-important job interview.

First, answer all questions briefly. When it comes to talking during an interview, less is more. As a general rule, you should speak one-third of the time and definitely no more than half of the time.

Second, remember that it's okay to be nervous. Actually, this is essential. Telling yourself you should feel differently than you do is unrealistic and makes you feel bad about yourself. Try to look at the process as a learning experience.

Third, be emotionally prepared. The right mood helps you perform at your best. Go for a walk, run, exercise, meditate, do yoga, stretch—anything to get the blood flowing to your brain. Try singing your favorite song while driving to the interview, repeating an inspirational phrase aloud that is meaningful for you, or simply remembering a time when you felt terrific.

Fourth, explain why you left your last job. Succinctly describe the reason for your departure, but do not go into details unless asked. Stay with the facts of what happened, what you did, how you felt, and what you learned. Then describe how you will handle things differently in the future. (Joseph should probably avoid the scorned wives of high-ranking governmental officials.)

Fifth, look better and you'll feel better. If you want to spruce up your appearance for the interview but can't afford new clothes, consider altering an outfit you already have by pairing it with a different shirt, tie, blouse, or accessory. Even on a tight budget, you can find good bargains. For better or worse, looks can make a difference.

Joseph was on his way to the biggest job interview of his life—an interview with the pharaoh of Egypt. He had everything against him. He was a foreigner in a foreign land. He was young with no bureaucratic or governmental experience. He had a shady past with a public scandal of sexual battery. He had a prison record. He had never visited Monster.com.

Further, to perform in a manner displeasing to Pharaoh could mean more than employment-related rejection. It could mean his neck in a noose. Joseph needed a lot more than tips from a website advice column. So he left his prison cell in a change of clothes and with a fresh shave (at least he followed one of the suggestions), not knowing what lay before him.

When Joseph arrived at the palace, Pharaoh cut to the chase: "Then Pharaoh said to Joseph, 'I had a dream last night, and no one here can tell me what it means. But I have heard that when you hear about a dream you can interpret it'" (Gen 41:15).

Joseph, following Monster's tips it seems, answered concisely: "It is beyond my power to do this, but God can tell you what it means and set you at ease" (Gen 41:16).

Joseph's opening phrase is a single word in the Hebrew text. It was an abrupt, terribly short answer. Yet, it was equally wise. It was true. Joseph could not answer Pharaoh. This was a task only God could perform.

Pharaoh recounted his dream for the Hebrew oracle.

So Pharaoh told Joseph his dream. "In my dream," he said, "I was standing on the bank of the Nile River, and I saw seven fat, healthy cows come up out of the river and begin grazing in the marsh grass. But then I saw seven sick-looking cows, scrawny and thin, come up after them. I've never seen such sorry-looking animals in all the land of Egypt. These thin, scrawny cows ate the seven fat cows. But afterward you wouldn't have known it, for they were still as thin and scrawny as before! Then I woke up.

"Then I fell asleep again, and I had another dream. This time I saw seven heads of grain, full and beautiful, growing on a single stalk. Then seven more heads of grain appeared, but these were blighted, shriveled, and withered by the east wind. And the shriveled heads swallowed the seven healthy heads. I told these dreams to the magicians, but no one could tell me what they mean." (Gen 41:17-24)

Joseph's interpretation, amazingly enough, followed immediately.

Joseph responded, "Both of Pharaoh's dreams mean the same thing. God is telling Pharaoh in advance what he is about to do. The seven healthy cows and the seven healthy heads of grain both represent seven years of prosperity. The seven thin, scrawny cows that came up later and the seven thin heads of grain, withered by the east wind, represent seven years of famine.

"This will happen just as I have described it, for God has revealed to Pharaoh in advance what he is about to do. The next seven years will be a period of great prosperity throughout the land of Egypt. But afterward there will be seven years of famine so great that all the prosperity will be forgotten in Egypt. Famine will destroy the land. This famine will be so severe that even the memory of the good years will be erased. As for having two similar dreams, it means that these events have been decreed by God, and he will soon make them happen." (Gen 41:25-32)

Egypt survived on two narrow strips of farmable land on either bank of the Nile River. Practically all Egyptian farming took place within these slivers of rich earth. Beyond these farmlands lay endless seas of sand and desert. The river would flood annually, the "gift of the Nile" it was called, in late summer and it would continue into early winter. Farming was impossible during these months.

This was a small price to pay. For when the Nile receded, it left in its wake a thick layer of fertile silt from the African heartland. Egyptian farmers took further advantage of this annual flood through an extensive network of trenches and irrigation canals. For a country that averaged less than two inches of rain a year, this flood-driven silt was the lifeblood of Egyptian agriculture and society. Without it, Egypt would have been a wasteland.

The Nile would rise more than twenty feet at flood time. If the flood was lower than expected, the sowing and reaping of crops would be mediocre at best, incapable of sustaining the country. If the Nile rose higher than expected it might damage a few Egyptian villages, but the crop production would be exceptional. The Egyptians carried on this agricultural dance with the river and soil with great skill, raising an incredible variety of crops in the desert sand.

Corn, emmer, and barley were the grains of choice for the climate. Onions, beans, lettuce, and cabbage flourished as well. The Egyptians were accomplished enough not only to support themselves, but to have excess production to store in granaries or export to neighboring countries.

As a result of these skills, prosperity was common in Egypt. It was as certain as the annual floods of the Nile. Famine—extensive famine—however, was unusual. This interpretation of Pharaoh's dream was, consequently, alarming. God was showing Pharaoh that the regular rise and fall of the Nile would certainly continue, but with extreme outcomes.

For seven years the flood would be massive, leading to bumper crop yields. This would be followed by seven years of insufficient flooding, resulting in famine. Without the proper planning, death would come to the entire nation. What Egypt needed was the execution of a masterful plan, a plan to use the years of abundance for the maximum benefit.

Violating the first rule of a good job interview, Joseph volunteered just such a plan. He said,

> "Therefore, Pharaoh should find an intelligent and wise man and put him in charge of the entire land of Egypt. Then Pharaoh should appoint supervisors over the land and let them collect one-fifth of all the crops during the seven good years. Have them gather all the food produced in the good years that are just ahead and bring it to Pharaoh's storehouses. Store it

away, and guard it so there will be food in the cities. That way there will be enough to eat when the seven years of famine come to the land of Egypt. Otherwise this famine will destroy the land." (Gen 41:33-36)

Joseph once had the habit of speaking too much. Such recklessness got him into his Egyptian calamity in the first place. But his free-flowing speech didn't hurt him this time.

His frank conversation with Pharaoh was the end to years of frustration and injustice. In a remarkable turn of events, Pharaoh concurred with Joseph's assessment and chose him to implement the strategy to save Egypt.

Joseph's suggestions were well received by Pharaoh and his officials. So Pharaoh asked his officials, "Can we find anyone else like this man so obviously filled with the spirit of God?" Then Pharaoh said to Joseph, "Since God has revealed the meaning of the dreams to you, clearly no one else is as intelligent or wise as you are. You will be in charge of my court, and all my people will take orders from you. Only I, sitting on my throne, will have a rank higher than yours."

Pharaoh said to Joseph, "I hereby put you in charge of the entire land of Egypt." Then Pharaoh removed his signet ring from his hand and placed it on Joseph's finger. He dressed him in fine linen clothing and hung a gold chain around his neck. Then he had Joseph ride in the chariot reserved for his second-in-command. And wherever Joseph went, the command was shouted, "Kneel down!" So Pharaoh put Joseph in charge of all Egypt. And Pharaoh said to him, "I am Pharaoh, but no one will lift a hand or foot in the entire land of Egypt without your approval." (Gen 41:37-44)

Drawing from his Arkansas roots, former president Bill Clinton often said, "If you see a turtle on a fence post, chances are it didn't get there by accident." What happened in Pharaoh's palace was no chance occurrence.

Joseph had been extensively prepared for this moment. Betrayed by his brothers and forced to live as a slave and a prisoner, he no doubt developed great compassion for the suffering, having felt his own stomach convulse with hunger more than once.

In Potiphar's house and in prison he had picked up the language and customs of Egypt, interacting with political prisoners and learning from their mistakes. His administrative skills had emerged, developed, and been honed to laser precision.

It had been an agonizing process, but there is no abbreviated course for greatness. Preparation is painful. Joseph's uniquely crafted experience equipped him for the task at hand. Who could do better than Joseph? At this specific time, no one. He was the right man in the right place at the right time.

But more was at play here: Joseph arrived at the pinnacle of world power with an intense spirituality. God's presence was gushing out of him. This was evident to all. It was clearly God's hand that had brought Joseph out of the hell of his existence to this elevated status. Joseph was on top of the fence post—on top of the world—and God had placed him there.

It is difficult to find a contemporary example of this kind of providential destiny. The closest example from our American heritage is probably Abraham Lincoln.

Young Lincoln did not spend his childhood in a romanticized Illinois log cabin. It was more like a lean-to. In the cold Midwestern winters, his family would huddle around a meager fire, too poor to buy basic staples. The Lincolns survived on what they could catch, kill, or pick. Things certainly did not improve for young Abe when his mother died. He was only nine years old. He went to work to help support the family.

His formal education was as sparse as his family's kitchen pantry. He received only one year of schoolroom teaching and was forced to rely upon his wit, ingenuity, and curiosity to supplement his learning. He often made his own handwritten copies of books or memorized borrowed volumes, reading greedily anything he could get his hands on.

Even as a child it appeared the Divine was inexplicably pushing Lincoln to greatness. The adversity of his early life seemed to bring out the best in him rather than serve as the deathblow to his will and spirit.

As an adult he held a variety of jobs. Persisting in his self-education, he became a lawyer and in 1852 entered the Illinois legislature. In 1860 Lincoln was elected president. He was just in his early fifties, and to the casual observer was nothing but a success. But his five-plus decades held incredible sufferings and crushing setbacks.

In addition to enduring his mother's death, Lincoln lost his fiancée to typhoid, married a woman who was declared insane, went bankrupt, lost eight different elections, suffered an emotional breakdown, and failed in business on numerous occasions.

The adversity of the years had prepared Lincoln to wrestle with the single greatest challenge the United States has ever faced: slavery and the dissolution of the Union. Lincoln committed to eradicating slavery and saving the nation at all costs. In 1861 the Civil War began. When it ended, Lincoln was still standing. While the country was laid waste by war, it too had survived and American slavery was no more. Lincoln was the right man in the right place at the right time, presiding over the most society-altering years in American history.

Then, like a character in some tragic novel, Lincoln entered the theater with his wife on Good Friday, 1865. As if his work was complete, he was gunned down by John Wilkes Booth. The curtain dropped on his life, and his iconic status was solidified for all of history.

Two days later—Passover and Easter—pastors, priests, and rabbis preached sermons and delivered homilies comparing the fallen president to Christ and Moses. He had brought the people out of bondage. He had died for the sins of slavery. He was the lawgiver and savior of the Union. It seems that Abraham Lincoln was uniquely prepared for the task of salvaging the nation.

Chapter after chapter, the writer of Genesis has built Joseph's story to this moment. Then, with just a few strokes of the pen, he summarizes the radical transition Joseph experiences. Included in this hasty summation are Joseph's marriage and the birth of his children. As Joseph exchanges the life of a Hebrew slave and prisoner for royalty, he also receives a name change from Pharaoh.

Pharaoh renamed Joseph *Zaphenath-paneah*. The name may mean "God speaks and lives" or "God the living One has spoken." The exact meaning of Joseph's name is lost to the sands of Egypt, but not so the names of his children. Of great significance are the names given to these two boys.

In the ancient cultures of the Near Mideast, names of children, or name changes as an adult, were important. Consider the meanings and circumstances surrounding the names given to Joseph's own brothers.

Joseph maintained this Hebrew custom with his own children. The firstborn he called "Manasseh," for "God has made me forget all my troubles and the family of my father" (Gen 41:51). The second he named "Ephraim," for "God has made me fruitful in this land of my suffering" (Gen 41:52).

Manasseh seemed to close the book on Joseph's past. He forgot his troubles. Of course, this doesn't mean his memory banks had been miraculously erased. How I wish this were possible. Simply, the memories and past injustices had begun to lose their sting and bitterness. The scars were still there. They always would be, but they were no longer quite as streaked with tenderness. Joseph was healing.

If Manasseh closed one chapter of Joseph's life, then Ephraim, the second born, opened a new one. The name "Ephraim" literally means "twice fruitful." As with the acidic and dry soil of the Nile valley, God refreshed Joseph with the rising flood of grace, allowing fruitfulness to burst forth in the desert. This land of arid suffering was now, for Joseph, an oasis that rivaled Eden itself.

As predicted, the years of plenty came. These were followed by famine, but Egypt was prepared. Joseph opened the granaries that held the bounty of seven good years and sold grain to the Egyptians. But the famine was not merely local. It was regional. With well-placed foreshadowing, the writer of Genesis states that people from the surrounding lands came to Egypt to buy grain as well. This stream of people included Joseph's brothers.

Just at the moment when Joseph's life reached a state of harmony, it was overturned again. This time it would not be upended by injustice but by the emotional turmoil of facing the men who had sold him into slavery as a teenager.

Joseph's story is not over. In some ways, it is just beginning.

Questions for Reflection

1. Joseph tells Pharaoh rather quickly that he does not have the power to interpret dreams. From where did Joseph's ability come? Why do you think Joseph was given this gift?

2. When Joseph proposed the plan to save Egypt, do you think he was thinking of himself as the one who would fill the job? Why or why not?

3. "Joseph's rise to success involved an agonizing process, but there is no abbreviated course for greatness. Preparation is painful." Some individuals are referred to as "natural-born leaders." Is this an accurate description, or do all leaders require extensive preparation?

4. Do you agree with the comparison of Joseph's life and preparation to the life and hardships of Abraham Lincoln? Are there others you can think of who seemed to be prepared for a difficult task by living through equally difficult times?

5. Joseph's children, Manasseh and Ephraim, were eventually adopted by their grandfather, Jacob. These two boys were given blessings and inheritance as if they were Jacob's own sons (see Gen 48:1-9). Why do you think Jacob did this?

6. For which do you think Joseph was better prepared—for saving Egypt from starvation or forgiving his brothers?

Sweet Dreams Are Made of These

If you don't have a dream, how can you have a dream come true?
—Jiminy Cricket

Students in a college English 101 class were asked to write a concise essay containing four key elements: religion, royalty, sex, and mystery. Points would be given for brevity without sacrificing substance. In other words, the shorter the better. The only A+ given in the class went to a story with a mere dozen words. It read, "'My God,' said the Queen, 'I'm pregnant! I wonder who did it.'"[1]

Sometimes an economy of words is best.

Genesis 42 opens with nine verses containing enough emotional conflict, innuendo, and unresolved transgression to fill a library. In simple, matter-of-fact language the author of the Genesis narrative skillfully changes the setting and scenery from Egypt to Palestine and back to Egypt.

In the process he yanks back the curtain on twenty years of shame. If the story of Joseph were a movie, here the camera would turn from his ordered life as governor over the land of the Nile to the chaos of starving Canaan.

The account reads,

> When Jacob heard that grain was available in Egypt, he said to his sons, "Why are you standing around looking at one another? I have heard there is grain in Egypt. Go down there, and buy enough grain to keep us alive. Otherwise we'll die."
>
> So Joseph's ten older brothers went down to Egypt to buy grain. But Jacob wouldn't let Joseph's younger brother, Benjamin, go with them, for

fear some harm might come to him. So Jacob's sons arrived in Egypt along with others to buy food, for the famine was in Canaan as well.

Since Joseph was governor of all Egypt and in charge of selling grain to all the people, it was to him that his brothers came. When they arrived, they bowed before him with their faces to the ground. Joseph recognized his brothers instantly, but he pretended to be a stranger and spoke harshly to them. "Where are you from?" he demanded.

"From the land of Canaan," they replied. "We have come to buy food."

Although Joseph recognized his brothers, they didn't recognize him. And he remembered the dreams he'd had about them many years before. (Gen 42:1-9a)

The hungry family of Jacob was so desperate for food that Jacob sent his sons into the forbidden land of Egypt to buy grain. But not all of them made the journey. Benjamin, maybe thirty years old now, stayed behind. Why? The text says it was fear of harm coming to Benjamin that led Jacob to this decision.

What harm? Was Jacob concerned about a horrible accident befalling his youngest son, the same fate as he was led to believe happened to Joseph? Maybe. Did it terrify Jacob to think of his youngest, now likely favored child entering the dangerous home of the pharaohs? Probably. Could Jacob be clinging to Benjamin as the only piece of Rachel and Joseph he had left? Perhaps.

Had twenty years of guilty consciences, whispered conversations, and averted gazes revealed the cold hard truth of what had really happened to Joseph? It is likely. Jacob was not about to send another favored son on an errand with this band of betrayers.

With the equivalent of a swift kick to the seat of their britches, the sons of Jacob, minus one, headed for Egypt. They blew into Joseph's life like a sirocco out of the desert. Joseph was engaged in one of the largest disaster relief projects in history, but now his energies would be diverted to the past, to the hurts that lay beneath the emotional surface, to these middle-aged graying men gathered in his palace.

The painful sentiments no doubt came flooding back in an instant. The nearly forgotten smell of the sheepfold and the tents of home filled his nostrils. He recalled the sweet, doting love of his father. He thought of his little brother Benjamin, wondering with a brief panic why he wasn't now among this group. He remembered the day his life changed, when these very men cast him into a cistern, cast him out of their lives, and robbed him of the years of his youth.

It happens to us all the time. The first familiar notes of a song, the scent of a particular cologne, the way the sun sets during a season of the year—these can all trigger memories, painful or pleasant, of events far in the past. They become as vivid as this morning's breakfast. Joseph's memories were staring him in the face.

Well, not exactly. They were actually on their faces staring at the floor. Joseph remembered more than the pain of his past. He suddenly remembered the dreams of his adolescence, dreams about his brother's haystacks bowing before his, dreams about the celestial bodies paying homage to him. The interpretation was clear then—he, the spoiled child of favor, would rule over his family. Now those dreams, sweetly, had come true.

The Chinese teacher Confucius, or K'ung-fu-tzu, said, "I hear and I forget. I see and I remember. I do and I understand."[2] Stories like that of Joseph take us past being an observer or a hearer. Stories like his force us into participation.

We put ourselves in his shoes, in the shoes of his brothers, or in the place of his father. Here, it is his brothers we must become. They are about to learn a great deal. We must learn with them. After all, life is too short to make all the possible mistakes ourselves. We need to learn from others' mistakes as well. It's possible to learn a great deal from these men in their early interactions with Joseph. We can go with them—do with them—and, along the way, understand.

Joseph began a kind of game with his unsuspecting brothers. They were easy targets. Fearful, huddled on the stone floor, they likely thought Joseph had been dead for years. For his part, Joseph would have borne all the outward signs of Egyptian royalty: a shaved head, white linen clothing, heavily lined eyes, speaking the Egyptian dialect with no hint of a Hebrew accent. With all this and twenty difficult years of living masking his face, he was completely unrecognizable.

This game was not intended to punish his brothers, for Joseph's kindness becomes clearer as the story continues to build toward a climax. This charade was a test. Joseph aimed to discover if these rascals had changed. Had the years transformed their character or were they still untrustworthy scoundrels, eaten up with envy and selfishness?

Three different times Joseph accused his brothers of being spies (Gen 42:9, 12, and 14) and threw them into jail for three days. They were incredulous and, ironically, appealed to their integrity as a defense: "Your servants are honest men," they replied. If only they had known who was hearing them plead their honest case. Joseph had once begged these men for mercy, for his life. Now those seeds sown in hostility were producing a bitter harvest.

Bowing in submission, servants to a foreign leader, the brothers begged for their lives, for mercy and understanding, in the very land to which they had sold their brother into slavery. As the pressure intensified around these men, they began to confess sins long kept secret. The first sin they acknowledged was their treatment of Joseph:

> Speaking among themselves, they said, "Clearly we are being punished because of what we did to Joseph long ago. We saw his anguish when he pleaded for his life, but we wouldn't listen. That's why we're in this trouble."
>
> "Didn't I tell you not to sin against the boy?" Reuben asked. "But you wouldn't listen. And now we have to answer for his blood!" (Gen 42:21-22)

Their crime, along with a sharp, well-placed "I told you so" from Reuben, returned to them with two decades' worth of interest on the principal. The biblical proverb, a person reaps what he sows, had become painfully obvious.

A few years ago John Matar stepped outside his Midwestern home to pick up the daily paper. It was his birthday, and he found two tons of cow manure piled eight feet high on his front lawn. The present, compliments of his brother in California, was the latest in an outlandish gift-giving war that had obviously gotten out of hand. It began between the two when John sent his sibling a particularly insulting birthday card. He got fifty cards back in return. The war was on.

John once received a pet rock that weighed more than two tons. He retaliated with ten tons of pebbles and pea gravel, and a note telling his brother that the pet rock had had babies. Gifts, if they can be called such, between the two have included a full-grown elephant and busloads of singing choirboys.[3] And to think, two tons of dung began with a single insult.

Joseph's brothers were soon up to their hip boots in dung themselves. Joseph kept one of his brothers, Simeon, as a prisoner in Egypt. The remaining brothers were graciously sent home with food but also with uncompromising instructions: "Bring your younger brother back to me to confirm your story. Failure to do this will prove your evil intentions as spies, and you will never see Simeon again."

This would be no easy task. Jacob would not let go of Benjamin easily, exclaiming,

> "You are robbing me of my children! Joseph is gone! Simeon is gone! And now you want to take Benjamin, too. Everything is going against me!
>
> My son will not go down with you. His brother Joseph is dead, and he is all I have left. If anything should happen to him on your journey, you would send this grieving, white-haired man to his grave." (Gen 42:36, 38)

Soon, though, the hunger pangs spoke louder than the protest. Jacob had to relent. After two years of stalling (I wonder how Simeon, sleeping every night in a Egyptian prison, felt about this delay), it was Judah who negotiated Benjamin's safe travel to Egypt.

> Judah said to his father, "Send the boy with me, and we will be on our way. Otherwise we will all die of starvation—and not only we, but you and our little ones. I personally guarantee his safety. You may hold me responsible if I don't bring him back to you. Then let me bear the blame forever. If we hadn't wasted all this time, we could have gone and returned twice by now."
>
> So their father, Jacob, finally said to them, "If it can't be avoided, then at least do this. Pack your bags with the best products of this land. Take them down to the man as gifts—balm, honey, gum, aromatic resin, pistachio nuts, and almonds. Also take double the money that was put back in your sacks, as it was probably someone's mistake [Joseph had put his brothers' first payment for grain back in their sacks making them appear as thieves]. Then take your brother, and go back to the man. May God Almighty give you mercy as you go before the man, so that he will release Simeon and let Benjamin return. But if I must lose my children, so be it."
>
> So the men packed Jacob's gifts and double the money and headed off with Benjamin. They finally arrived in Egypt and presented themselves to Joseph. (Gen 43:8-15)

You may remember that it was Judah who led the brotherly conspiracy against Joseph. Here, he offered himself as the guarantor of Benjamin's safety. He promised that no harm would befall him. Certainly this could be hunger speaking, desperate measures for desperate times. But it looks more like shades of maturity. Besides, since that fateful day when Joseph was sold into slavery, Judah had learned a great deal about deception, betrayal, and family turmoil himself.

Back in Genesis 38, we find an interruption in the account of Joseph's life. Chapter 37 closes with Joseph being sold into slavery. Chapter 39 resumes his story, finding him in Potiphar's house. Between these two chapters is a sordid tale that focuses exclusively on Judah. Genesis 38 gives possible insight to the changes we begin to see in his character.

Genesis 38 is one of those biblical stories that does not meet the PG-13 standard. It is a twisted, sexually charged yarn you might find more readily on the big screen of an American movie theater than in a holy book. As the story goes, Judah had married a Canaanite woman who bore him three sons. In time, Judah arranged a marriage for the oldest—a shiftless, evil young man named Er. His new wife was a woman called Tamar. The Bible says that following the wedding, Er was so wicked that God took his life.

Er's younger brother Onan refused to follow the ancient custom of taking in the widow of a brother as his own wife to perpetuate his brother's lineage. Onan was happy to have sex with Tamar, but refused her a pregnancy. Bluntly, the Bible says God took Onan's life as well.

This left Judah with one son, the youngest, Shelah. Judah promised Tamar that when this son was old enough to marry, Shelah would fulfill the ancient custom and become her husband. Tamar no doubt longed for that day. For a Middle Eastern woman living in ancient days, there was no greater shame or greater economic tragedy than being left without husband and heir. In this paternalistic culture of the past, such a woman was left without resource or justice.

Regretfully, Judah's promise was a farce. He feared for Shelah's life. This woman had taken two sons already. He would not let her have the third one. Maybe Judah felt the same paternal angst and pain he had inflicted upon his own father. Maybe through the stress of protecting a young favored son, he gained a new perspective on his father's behavior. Maybe this experience of burying his own children shook him at his core. He definitely behaved differently following these events.

The years passed and Shelah was never given to Tamar. Judah would not keep his promise, exploiting Tamar's vulnerable position. Being an enterprising woman, however, she took matters into her own hands. Disguised, she positioned herself along a busy highway where she knew Judah would pass on his way to shear his sheep. But she was not there to watch a parade of smelly shepherds or to pass the afternoon. Instead, she presented herself as a prostitute and successfully lured Judah into her bed.

When the transaction was complete, Tamar demanded a pledge that Judah would in fact pay her for the night of pleasure. Judah left his seal, chord, and walking stick with her, promising the payment of a young goat. Incredible as it may seem, for the time period this appears to have been a fair payment. This seal, chord, and walking stick were as unique as a Social Security number, a driver's license, or a fingerprint. There could be no doubt as to who these items belonged.

Months later it became obvious to everyone that Tamar was pregnant. Without a husband, the right conclusion was drawn that she had prostituted herself. When informed of his daughter-in-law's indiscretion, Judah was furious. Full of righteous indignation, he demanded her execution. As she was being carried to the site of her stoning and eventual burning, she produced the seal, chord, and walking stick as identification of the father of the twins now wrestling in her womb.

Judah was then forced to acknowledge publicly his own guilt, the failure to keep his word, and Tamar's enterprising, though unorthodox virtue. Judah, finding himself on the receiving end of manipulation and deception, could not have liked the way it felt. This whole series of events seemed to change him. At the very least, it began the process.

But the real test of Judah's character change lay not in the past, but ahead of him in Egypt. He and his brothers returned to Egypt, driven by hunger, and once again bowed before Joseph. For his part, Joseph had had months to revisit his pain and resurrect his grievances. With Benjamin now safely under his roof, Joseph could take his revenge against the others and right the wrongs of two decades. Instead, he threw a party.

Genesis 43:24-25 says, "The manager then led the men into Joseph's palace. He gave them water to wash their feet and provided food for their donkeys. They were told they would be eating there, so they prepared their gifts for Joseph's arrival at noon."

Do you know why most of us do not take revenge against those who have harmed us? We can't. We are not deterred from taking our retaliation by the law or our good nature or some internal moral code. Instead, we are prevented from taking revenge by time, by distance, or by circumstances. We cannot reach that person or persons who have hurt us. The ones we wish we could punish hold so much power, authority, or money that they are untouchable. Maybe they have already died, moved, or vanished. Those who robbed us of something valuable—our innocence, our time, our fortune, our dreams—escape justice and we have no recourse to make things right.

Steven Spielberg's 1993 masterpiece *Schindler's List* is likely the greatest American retelling of the Jewish Holocaust. Based on the real life of German industrialist Oskar Schindler, the movie follows his efforts to rescue more than a thousand would-be victims of German atrocities. While those on Schindler's worker list and in his manufacturing plants suffered greatly, they were saved from being shipped to work camps and liquidation sites like Auschwitz. More than 6,000 descendants of these workers owe their lives to this man who risked his own life and lost his fortune in the process of protecting them.

Schindler, complexly portrayed by actor Liam Neeson, developed a tenuous friendship with the German commandant over the Plaszow Labor Camp, Amon Goeth. Goeth is ruthless, the epitome of Nazi cruelty. In one unsettling scene in the film, Goeth marshals his rifle for target practice. From the balcony of his hilltop villa he looks through the high-powered scope at one unsuspecting person after another. He shoots and kills at leisure.

Later, on this same balcony, Schindler joins Goeth after a villa party. A drunken Goeth receives something of a sermon from Schindler that is one of the more insightful exchanges in the movie.

Goeth: You know, I look at you. I watch you. You're not a drunk. That's, that's real control. Control is power. That's power.
Schindler: Is that why they fear us?
Goeth: We have the . . . power to kill, that's why they fear us.
Schindler: They fear us because we have the power to kill arbitrarily. A man commits a crime, he should know better. We have him killed and we feel pretty good about it. Or we kill him ourselves and we feel even better. That's not power, though, that's justice. That's different than power. Power is when we have every justification to kill—and we don't.
Goeth: You think that's power?
Schindler: That's what the emperors had. A man stole something, he's brought in before the emperor, he throws himself down on the ground, he begs for mercy, he knows he's going to die. And the emperor pardons him. This worthless man, he lets him go.
Goeth: I think you are drunk.
Schindler: That's power, Amon. That is power.[4]

Later, Goeth browbeats a stable boy for failing to store properly his expensive riding saddle, a gift given by Schindler. But in a change of character, Goeth forgives rather than beat or kill the young man. In camp that same afternoon, he pardons a woman prisoner caught smoking on the job. Still later, in his villa, the same stable boy is unable to remove stains from the bathtub. Amon Goeth takes what appears to be a labored breath, taps the boy on the shoulder, and says, "Go ahead, go on leave. I pardon you."

Goeth's pardon is short lived, and so is Schindler's sermon. The stable boy is the next victim caught in the crosshairs of the commandant's rifle. For Goeth, killing Jews from his villa balcony was more satisfying—more powerful—than pardon.

Joseph, like Amon Goeth, was not in the frustrating position of powerlessness. He held both the ability and opportunity to punish those who had hurt him. In a moment he could have summoned a cohort of Egyptian soldiers into his palace and executed his offenders under the pretense that they were spies. He could have erased their names and their futures in an instant. Yet he refused to do so.

It foreshadowed a day when Christ would hang on a Roman cross, jeered at and slandered by the crowds. The great power of the crucifixion moment was not just in Christ's sufferings for his creation. The greatness of that moment was crystallized in the fact that he could have asked his "Father for thousands of angels . . . and he would send them instantly" (Matt 26:53). Yet he too refused to do so. He did not retaliate or "threaten revenge when he suffered. He left his case in the hands of God, who always judges fairly" (1 Pet 2:23).

To have the ability to take vengeance is a power of sorts, a power we often wish we had. But to have the ability and refuse to use it—that is real power.

Questions for Reflection

1. Jacob protested Benjamin's journey to Egypt. I have suggested it is because Jacob had learned what had actually happened to Joseph. Do you agree or disagree? For what other reasons would Jacob not want Benjamin to go to Egypt?

2. Joseph was painfully confronted with the men and memories of the past. Has there ever been a time in your life when you had to confront painful memories or circumstances?

3. Confucius said, "I hear and I forget. I see and I remember. I do and I understand." Does this ring true in your own experience? How can we "do" or live out the biblical stories in such a way that we truly begin to understand?

4. Joseph played a kind of game with his brothers that included deliberate deception. Was this the right thing to do? Why or why not?

5. Judah, the lead conspirator against Joseph, was later forced to bury two sons of his own. Do you think this is what changed his attitude toward his father and what he had done to Joseph?

6. "To have the ability to take vengeance is a power of sorts, a power we often wish we had. But to have the ability and refuse to use it—that is real power." Do you agree with this statement? Why or why not?

Notes

[1] E. T. Thompson, *Reader's Digest,* July 2003, 32.

[2] As quoted by Larry G. Peppers, *Simulated Society* (SIMSOC) *Module,* Gordon County Chamber of Commerce Leadership Retreat, Marietta GA, 17 January 2004.

[3] *Campus Life,* January 1980, 22.

[4] *Schindler's List,* written by Thomas Keneally and Steven Zaillian, dir. Steven Spielberg, Universal Studios, 1993.

The Best-laid Plan

Two things are infinite: the universe and human stupidity; and I'm not sure about the universe. — Albert Einstein

On April 24, 1915, the Turkish government arrested scores of Armenian poets, intellectuals, and religious and community leaders in Constantinople. Draped by the chaos of World War I, these men and women were then deported into Anatolia and put to death. So began the twentieth century's first, and largely forgotten, genocide. Before the atrocities ended, almost two million Armenians were murdered, raped, or deported.

Following this initial strike, the Turks systematically removed able-bodied men from their communities under the guise of a draft for the war effort. These men were killed or worked to death in faraway labor camps. The remaining women, children, and elderly were death-marched into the Syrian Desert and intentionally left without food and water.

National, religious, and cultural landmarks were obliterated. Armenian children were abducted, their names were changed, and they were given to Turks. The corpses of the fallen littered the Ottoman highways. The result was the near extinction of a culture thousands of years old.

Gournig Yankian, a youngster at the time, was among those at the receiving end of Turkish brutality. He witnessed the horrific murder of his brother, but he somehow survived the genocide himself. After the war he refused to take revenge against those who had robbed him of his family. Eventually he left Europe and immigrated to America. In the States, Yankian wrote books about the atrocities he had witnessed, serving as a voice to

awaken the world's conscience. In time he achieved a life of respectable nor-
malcy.

In 1973, almost six decades after his sufferings, he invited two Turkish
diplomats to a meeting in his hotel room, ostensibly to present them with
two rare paintings, an "act of good will." Upon their arrival, he coolly executed them both. Then he put down his pistol, called the authorities, and
confessed to the crime.

More than revenge motivated him. He committed the murders in an
attempt to stop the nightmares he had experienced since his brother's death.
These nightmares visited him regularly and were driven, he concluded, by
his failure to avenge his brother's death. It appears to have worked. Before his
death in 1984, Yankian claimed that the assassinations had in fact cured him
of those terrible dreams. He never lost a minute's sleep over the death of his
brother again.[1]

A clear conscience is a soft pillow, but is the cleansing of the conscience
best achieved by unjust means?

Also a victim of deportation and injustice, our friend Joseph would have
easily identified with Gournig Yankian. His family was taken away from
him. He too had been abducted and then cast aside in the desert. He had
been imprisoned, forgotten, and abandoned. Years later, he too had the
opportunity to plot his revenge.

In Genesis 44, Joseph's tangled plot reaches its climax. This plot is not
one of revenge, but it is a test: have Joseph's brothers changed? Are these the
same conniving criminals of two decades earlier? Will they abandon another
brother to Egypt? These are the questions that robbed Joseph of sleep. He
made a great effort to find the answers, and one would be hard pressed to
find a more ingenious dragnet anywhere than this well-laid plan of Joseph.

After feasting with his brothers, reuniting with Benjamin, and loading
their donkeys with precious Egyptian grain, he turned up the heat a final
time. Joseph instructs his palace manager to put each of his brothers' money
back into the feed sacks they had just purchased. Then, he was to put
Joseph's personal cup—a valued symbol of his authority—into Benjamin's
sack. Joseph allows his brothers to get just outside the shadow of his palace
before springing the trap:

> Joseph said to his palace manager, "Chase after them and stop them. When
> you catch up with them, ask them, 'Why have you repaid my kindness
> with such evil? Why have you stolen my master's silver cup, which he uses
> to predict the future? What a wicked thing you have done!'"

When the palace manager caught up with the men, he spoke to them as he had been instructed.

"What are you talking about?" the brothers responded. "We are your servants and would never do such a thing! Didn't we return the money we found in our sacks? We brought it back all the way from the land of Canaan. Why would we steal silver or gold from your master's house? If you find his cup with any one of us, let that man die. And all the rest of us, my lord, will be your slaves."

"That's fair," the man replied. "But only the one who stole the cup will be my slave. The rest of you may go free."

They all quickly took their sacks from the backs of their donkeys and opened them. The palace manager searched the brothers' sacks, from the oldest to the youngest. And the cup was found in Benjamin's sack! When the brothers saw this, they tore their clothing in despair. Then they loaded their donkeys again and returned to the city. (Gen 44:1-13)

Joseph's brothers were forced to play out their hand in this unusual game. The deck was stacked against them. They were now accused and condemned of a crime they did not commit. They had consigned themselves as slaves in Egypt, and they had an opportunity to scapegoat the younger brother, Benjamin, to escape. The parallels within Joseph's plan are obvious. A skillful actor, Joseph played his part well.

Joseph was still in his palace when Judah and his brothers arrived, and they fell to the ground before him. "What have you done?" Joseph demanded. "Don't you know that a man like me can predict the future?"

Judah answered, "Oh, my lord, what can we say to you? How can we explain this? How can we prove our innocence? God is punishing us for our sins. My lord, we have all returned to be your slaves— all of us, not just our brother who had your cup in his sack."

"No," Joseph said. "I would never do such a thing! Only the man who stole the cup will be my slave. The rest of you may go back to your father in peace." (Gen 44:14-17)

For a fourth time the brothers fulfilled the dreams of Joseph's adolescence. They fell on their faces before him. There on the palace floor they found themselves painted into a corner. Benjamin's presence had been demanded in Egypt, and in spite of the dangers, they had brought him, resulting in the release of Simeon. Then, at the previous evening's feast, Benjamin had been obviously favored, receiving a meal portion five times what the others had received (Gen 43:34). Now, Benjamin was apparently responsible for the disaster that had befallen them.

Joseph's silver cup had been found in Benjamin's possession, and the punishment for his thievery, though to be death initially, was a life of slavery in Egypt. The rest of the brothers would be allowed to return to Canaan in peace, just as they had returned to their father so many years earlier.

Every conspiracy, from the Enron debacle to local political disasters, needs a fall guy. Joseph delivered Benjamin to his brothers in a silver cup. Would they abandon Benjamin as they had once abandoned Joseph? Would they take the easy way out to save their own necks? Would they once again deliver the news of a favored son's disappearance?

One of the more famous scapegoats in American history is Admiral Husband E. Kimmel. He commanded the Pacific Fleet based at Pearl Harbor when Japanese dive-bombers and torpedo planes attacked Hawaii on December 7, 1941. When the Japanese completed their attack, eighteen naval vessels were damaged or lying at the bottom of the harbor. Almost 400 planes were destroyed or damaged, and, most disastrous, more than 2,000 service men and women died. The U.S. public cried out for vengeance.

In the rush to judgment, the Roberts Commission, chaired by then Supreme Court justice Owen J. Roberts, was formed within days of the attack. The commission concluded that Kimmel, along with Army General Walter C. Short, was guilty of dereliction of duty. Kimmel was immediately relieved of his command, charged with being unprepared for the attack, and disgracefully demoted. Worse, he was shamed for the rest of his life.

Personally bearing the humiliation of a national failure, he often concluded that it would have been better if he had died at Pearl Harbor. He lived until 1968 still laboring to clear his name of the burden placed upon him.

Historical perspective has achieved for Kimmel what he could not achieve for himself. He has been largely vindicated of sole responsibility for the Pearl Harbor attack. While he and others in command at Pearl Harbor should have been more alert to the Japanese danger, all investigations beyond the Roberts Commission concluded that he acted professionally and appropriately.

Washington D.C. and the army and naval leadership all knew of Japan's intentions well before the attack, but the bureaucratic-laden structure failed to communicate the necessary intelligence and warnings to Kimmel in the field. Further, American policy at the time invited a war with Japan as a means of rallying to the Allies in Europe. But President Franklin D. Roosevelt waited for an attack, refusing to take the first shot.

It is naïve to think that the United States was simply minding its own business until Tokyo dragged America into the war. Events were much more complex than that. Responsibility for Pearl Harbor must be born by many, even those who were at the highest level of government. Still, Kimmel was an easy target.

Congress finally exonerated Kimmel and restored his rank in the year 2000, some sixty years after that "Day of Infamy." Though he did not live to see the day, for Kimmel, things were finally made right.

Joseph's brothers, in a sense, had that same chance—to make things right. Judah, who led the conspiracy against Joseph, was again the first to speak, but this time he showed no signs of abandoning Benjamin in Egypt. Instead, he offered himself.

> Then Judah stepped forward and said, "Please, my lord, let your servant say just one word to you. Please, do not be angry with me, even though you are as powerful as Pharaoh himself.
>
> "And now, my lord, I cannot go back to my father without the boy. Our father's life is bound up in the boy's life. If he sees that the boy is not with us, our father will die. We, your servants, will indeed be responsible for sending that grieving, white-haired man to his grave. My lord, I guaranteed to my father that I would take care of the boy. I told him, 'If I don't bring him back to you, I will bear the blame forever.'
>
> "So please, my lord, let me stay here as a slave instead of the boy, and let the boy return with his brothers. For how can I return to my father if the boy is not with me? I couldn't bear to see the anguish this would cause my father!" (Gen 44:18, 30-34)

Joseph's plan worked. Applying crucible-like pressure, he succeeded in squeezing out of his brothers what was in their hearts; hearts that had changed since their rash act of betrayal many years earlier. Judah, speaking for them all, could not bear the thought of once again inflicting upon his father the misery of a lost son. For decades he and his brothers had carried the guilt of their sin. Here, he refused to pick up that heavy load once again. He would rather spend the rest of his life as a slave in Egypt than lock himself in that prison of his own making.

Judah is a living example of what the Apostle Paul describes in 2 Corinthians 7. After Paul's painful visits and letters to the believers at

Corinth, his initial readers reached a place of repentance and remorse over their sins. He wrote out of "pure joy" that the painful path they had taken led them to a restored relationship with God and others. Paul concluded that there are two types of sorrow or grief. There is a pain that causes people "to repent and change" their ways. This kind of sorrow leads us "away from sin and results in salvation." There is also a worldly sorrow that lacks repentance, a sorrow that results in hopelessness, despair, and "spiritual death."

Maybe we can view it in this light: Good sorrow is like exercise. Vigorous exercise hurts. Your muscles burn, your head spins, your lungs become like a furnace burning coal, your heart pounds in your ears. You say to yourself, or at least I say to myself, "It would have been better to stay home, lying on the couch eating Fritos. Why am I doing this? This hurts!" It does hurt, but it is good for you. It is making you stronger, healthier, better. That is what good sorrow, good grief, does.

Bad sorrow, "sorrow of the world," Paul called it, is more like a heart attack. You get the same sensations: Your muscles burn, your head spins, your chest feels like an elephant is sitting on it, but this pain is not good for you. This pain is killing you. That is what bad sorrow, bad grief, does.

The contrast is sharp. Sorrow that leads us to repentance, to the open arms of God, brings us perspective, maturity, transformation, and a life without regret. Sorrow that leads us away from repentance and leads us to resist and even hate God brings us to regret and spiritual death.

We are all going to have regrets in some form or another, the "would-a, should-a, could-as."

I should have never married that man.

I should have never gotten behind the wheel that night.

If I had been thinking, I would have never signed that contract.

If only I could go back and change that one day, that one minute.

I would give anything to pull back those words.

The list is endless. You fill in the blank. We have regrets. What will we do with them?

A few years ago I sat at the bedside of an old man who was dying. Physically, he was a train wreck. I cannot begin to recall all the things that had gone wrong. It was as if his body was in rebellion against him—diabetes, heart troubles, respiratory issues, infection, on and on. To make matters worse, he was a hard man. He was rude to the medical staff. He was demanding. The only reason he accepted a visit from me is because, even in his compromised condition, he still wanted to debate—to fight—about religion.

It didn't take long, as we jousted back and forth, for our conversation to turn toward the end of life; toward the fact that this man's time was nearing an end. Tears welled in his eyes, and the hardened façade he had been maintaining began to crumble. He said, "I need to tell you something."

He took me back six decades to the French countryside. It was summer in the weeks following the D-Day invasion of Normandy. This old man was then a young soldier in communications, wanting to do his part for his country, but he never intended to point a gun or take a life. Yet he found himself forced into a situation.

A Hitler youth, a teenager maybe fifteen years old, had been taken captive behind the lines. Because he was the only one available and not an infantryman pushing toward the front lines, the man told me he was put in charge of holding this youth until he could be relieved. Unexpectedly, the young German boy produced a knife from his boot and attacked. In the ensuing struggle, the Hitler youth was killed. The old man completed his story by saying, "I have prayed for that boy's soul every day of my life."

By this time, those gigantic tears were rolling down his face and mine. His body shook with the sobbing. I feared for a moment that he was going to have a heart attack. The grief was so strong, and though it was sixty years old, it was still so fresh. The hard, thick hide and mean spirit was nothing more than the natural outcome of carrying grief and sorrow around for his entire life. But even as an old man, he let free the shame that was decades old.

Judah was choosing between these two types of grief. He could embrace his regret over what he did to Joseph, confess it, learn from it, and allow it to bring relief. Or he could follow the familiar path of betrayal and die the slow, painful death of the miserable. Judah made the wise choice.

Along with a dozen men and women from my church, I once traveled to an orphanage outside of La Esperanza, Honduras, to help with a construction project. Laboring with the Anglo missionaries and the locals, we made our own bricks and mortar; we raised walls; we laid pipe. We built a new structure that doubled the capacity of this little outpost of hope.

It was no simple task getting to our destination. Flying out of Atlanta, Georgia, is trouble enough, but once on the ground in Honduras, travel was much more difficult. It took more than six hours to travel a little more than a hundred miles on the primitive roads of Central America. At times our guide had to get out of our van and walk ahead, pointing out the worst ruts, plotting a course for the driver like bringing an airplane into a hangar. This exercise continued every few miles long after the sun had set.

Our guide got too far ahead of us at one point and was gone for what seemed an especially long time. He finally came staggering back into the headlights, bleeding, dazed, and battered. We jumped to the conclusion that he had been assaulted in the darkness, but when he climbed back into the van we realized how incorrect our assumption was. In addition to his injuries, he smelled like a sewer. In fact, that is exactly where he had been.

Scouting for ruts ahead in the dark, he had fallen five or so feet into a cesspit. It made the last hour to the orphanage a misery for all of us. Still, there was some humor in his little disaster. Through the blood and filth of his wounds, he uttered a profound phrase: "You got to be tough if you're gonna be stupid."

We start down certain paths knowing, but not admitting, the eventual outcome. Road signs the size of billboards might as well be pointing out the dangers. In the back of our minds we know it is going to hurt. Bad relationship choices, poor financial decisions, overly ambitious business goals, acts of selfishness and deceit: in the end we stagger out of the dark, bloodied and beaten, looking and smelling worse for the wear.

Making a few bad decisions is a part of living. You learn your lesson; you adjust and grow wiser as a result. I doubt that those who claim never to have made such decisions in life are actually living at all. But to continue to make bad decisions—one after the other—is a sign of our foolishness and requires a toughened resolve and even tougher skin, because it is going to hurt.

We humans have an almost infinite capacity for resisting what is best for us. We defiantly refuse repentance. We reject a change of direction for our lives. Thanks be to God, though, there is at least one thing stronger than fallen, human stubbornness: grace.

Grace is a necessary turnaround on a wrong-way street. Grace offers a detour off the path of destruction. God's grace provides the opportunity and power to truly, actually change.

Let there be no mistake. We are strong, but when up against an all-powerful God with inexhaustible mercy, time is on his side and our strength withers like grass in the summer heat. Still, God will not use that power and time to brutalize us by means of sheer muscle. Instead, God fiercely loves us into submission. The war we wage against him is a war against love, and, thankfully, love never fails—not even in the face of stupidity.

Musician Layton Howerton says it eloquently:

You finally broke me.
This time you really knocked me to my knees.
You got my attention.
You rung my bell, yeah you stung me like a bee.
And you got to know when to throw the towel in.
But I'm tired of pain and the taste of suffering;
Of blood and sweat when you get what's coming;
Of push and shove, of lacing up these gloves;
Of fisticuffs that test the stuff you're made of.
And I'll be thankful just to walk away,
From boxing with you God.
And live to fight another day.[2]

How long will you box with God over the direction of your life? How long will you hold on to your rebellion and selfishness? How far will you travel in the wrong direction? How much will you lose? How deeply will you hurt those who love you? How much misery will you inflict upon yourself?

Judah was at the end of his road, a road he had traveled for two decades. Having had enough, he turned around and headed for home.

Questions for Reflection

1. Gournig Yankian claimed to have cleared his conscience by killing two men. What convinces people that revenge will solve past injustices?

2. Do you think Joseph's brothers thought about offering Benjamin as the scapegoat to save their own necks? Why or why not? Had the brothers abandoned Benjamin, what do you think Joseph would have done?

3. Read 2 Corinthians 7:8-11. What is the difference between "godly sorrow" and "worldly sorrow"? Do you think Judah's pleadings before Joseph were a sign of remorse or repentance?

4. Do you believe "We humans have an almost infinite capacity for resisting what is best for us"? Why or why not?

5. Do you believe that God will love us into submission rather than using sheer muscle? Have you ever experienced God's "muscle" apart from God's love?

6. Much that is said about forgiveness is directed at individuals. Can repentance and the breaking of the cycle of revenge become reality for groups of people? For churches? For nations?

Notes

[1] James Hersh, "From *Ethnos* to *Polis*: The Furies and Apollo," *Spring* (April 1985): 57.

[2] Layton Howerton, "Boxing God," from *Boxing God*, Sparrow Records, January 1998.

Enough Blood and Tears

So I'm crying on a bench in an old time station; betting all I've got on forgiveness. —Mason Jennings

Charles Lowery tells the story of a husband and wife who reached an impasse in their marriage. Years of resentment and hurt had piled up until it threatened to smother the relationship. They made an appointment with a therapist. The therapist came to their home, sat in their living room, and began the tedious work of unpacking this couple's baggage.

It took some time to dig through it all, but finally the husband admitted that he was especially angry that in all their years of marriage his wife had never—never—changed the toilet tissue roll in the bathroom.

The wife was incredulous. She protested the accusation and countered that she had in fact changed the toilet paper roll countless times. The husband exploded in anger and stormed from the room. A few seconds later, he returned with several large plastic garbage bags he had been storing in his closet.

He ripped the bags open and began raining the contents all over the room. The bags were filled with hundreds of empty cardboard cylinders inscribed with a date and time. Through the years the husband had meticulously recorded and stockpiled every time he had changed the toilet paper roll.[1]

It is easy to keep a record of offenses. We all do it. We may not do it with the same neurosis of the husband with his toilet paper rolls, but we keep score nonetheless. We know who has hurt us. We know how we were hurt, and we know where and when it all happened. We keep a mental list of those who deserve retaliation, and we can recall the date, time, and place of the wrongdoing against us.

How can we rid ourselves of this kind of baggage, of this kind of heaviness? If there is a way to purge our insides of the hurt and bitterness of injustice against us, do we even want to do so? Sometimes we would rather coddle and nurse the wrongs committed against us than to do the necessary and difficult work of forgiving those who have harmed us.

It may be easy for those of us who call ourselves Christians to speak flippantly of forgiveness, but it is another thing altogether to actually forgive. Forgiveness, while liberating and healing to both the forgiver and forgiven, is a costly enterprise. No one could have known this better than Joseph.

As difficult as forgiveness is to grant, Joseph was willing to pay the price. Graciously, deliberately, and eagerly Joseph cut the chains of injustice and allowed his brothers to go free.

> Joseph could stand it no longer. There were many people in the room, and he said to his attendants, "Out, all of you!" So he was alone with his brothers when he told them who he was. Then he broke down and wept. He wept so loudly the Egyptians could hear him, and word of it quickly carried to Pharaoh's palace.
>
> "I am Joseph!" he said to his brothers. "Is my father still alive?" But his brothers were speechless! They were stunned to realize that Joseph was standing there in front of them. "Please, come closer," he said to them. So they came closer. And he said again, "I am Joseph, your brother, whom you sold into slavery in Egypt. But don't be upset, and don't be angry with yourselves for selling me to this place. It was God who sent me here ahead of you to preserve your lives."
>
> Then Joseph added, "Look! You can see for yourselves, and so can my brother Benjamin, that I really am Joseph! Go tell my father of my honored position here in Egypt. Describe for him everything you have seen, and then bring my father here quickly." Weeping with joy, he embraced Benjamin, and Benjamin did the same. Then Joseph kissed each of his brothers and wept over them, and after that they began talking freely with him. (Gen 45:1-5, 12-15)

It is impossible to capture the astonishment of these moments in Joseph's palace as he revealed his true identity to his brothers. The fierce ruler of Egypt was reduced to a weeping, wailing, emotional wreck, stuttering broken words in guttural Hebrew. The public image, so rigidly maintained over the last several years, came crashing down. With tears cascading off his cheeks, Zaphenath-paneah of Egypt revealed himself as Joseph of Canaan.

Gone was the strange, unintelligible dialect of northern Africa. Gone was the harshness and roughness of suspicion. These all washed away with the tears of grace and forgiveness. "I am Joseph!" There may be no more startling revelation anywhere else in the Hebrew literature.

Startling is an understatement for what Joseph's brothers now experienced. Like an apparition from the past or a terrible nightmare, the dreamer lorded over them as predicted. If they were afraid standing before the governor of Egypt, they were now terrified standing before Joseph. Physically they recoiled from his presence. The shock, the shame, the fear was too much to bear. Had they not been behind the closed doors of the palace, they certainly would have run for their lives.

But compassionately—miraculously—there was nothing to fear. Joseph greeted them, not with hate and judgment, but with kisses and tears. Joseph granted the most improbable of gifts: forgiveness.

Forgiveness is no easy thing; not for Joseph, not for anyone. Its difficulty lies in the fact that it is not natural. It is not fair. It deprives the one who has been offended—the victim—from achieving justice. Forgiveness lets the offender off the hook. It sets the offender free without penalty and without punishment for the sin he or she has committed.

The mere thought of this is enough to turn our stomachs. How can someone who has stolen from us, molested us, betrayed us, abused us—how can these people, these crimes, be forgiven? How can we open the door on the jail cell in which we hold them and simply allow them to walk away?

The answer is as complex as it is simple. Every time forgiveness takes place, the price for that offense is paid, but it is paid by the victim rather than the wrongdoer. When forgiveness is granted, the one who has been hurt is saying, "I will live with the consequences of what has happened without vengeance, without bitterness, and without the demand of payment. I will pay the price myself. I will absorb the loss."

As Joseph granted forgiveness to his brothers, he was essentially opening the ledger, marking their debts "paid in full," and then closing the account. He gave up his rights. He relinquished his need for compensation and personally bore the cost of their sin against himself. Every time the words "I forgive you" are spoken, this is the transaction that takes place.

One cannot speak of forgiveness without being driven to the words of Christ as he suffered upon the cross. "Father, forgive them," he prayed, "for they don't know what they are doing" (Luke 23:34). These words were not spoken in the warm light of hindsight. Jesus spoke them as the nails pierced his flesh, as the Roman iron ruptured muscle and arteries, as the cross was raised on the hill of the Skull and pain exploded in his body.

Jesus, a man of innocence, wrongly condemned, undeserving of the treatment of a criminal, did not curse his tormentors. Instead, he offered prayers of forgiveness. He prayed for the soldiers carrying out their orders. He prayed for the crowd of onlookers who easily joined in the heckling of the condemned. He prayed for the religious and civil authorities, Herod and Pilate, who sent Jesus to his death for the sake of political expediency. Jesus prayed for them all, asking his Father to forgive them.

When choosing to forgive, Jesus called on someone outside himself. He didn't say, "I forgive you," though he easily could have. He said, "Father, for-give them." Wrestling with this text, Ron Gaynor defines forgiveness as "a miracle of grace that God does through us."[2] It is not something we accom-plish on our own. God must do it for us and through us.

If we look to Jesus and Joseph as examples of forgiveness, their leader-ship inspiring us to follow suit, then we have captured only half of the forgiveness story. The source of their forgiveness is the more essential matter. Their forgiveness flowed from the reality that they had left their situation "in the hands of God, who always judges fairly" (1 Pet 2:23).

Joseph, likewise, came to understand this broader perspective and told his brothers, "God has sent me ahead of you to keep you and your families alive. . . . So it was God who sent me here, not you" (Gen 45:7-8).

If there is any chance of forgiving those who have hurt us, it will be because something otherworldly has taken over our hearts and minds. It will be because the Father has worked that miracle of grace in us and through us. Rather than trying to muster up forgiveness on our own, which we are truly incapable of doing, it is the better choice to ask God to do it for us. When God does, it is obvious to a watching world that something Divine is at work.

On Monday morning, October 2, 2006, Charles Roberts, a thirty-two-year-old Pennsylvanian milkman, prepared his children for school. He and his wife, Marie, got them dressed, fed them their breakfast, and hustled them to the bus stop. Marie then left for her regular prayer meeting.

Charles made his way to the West Nickel Mines Amish School. In his vehicle were multiple weapons, ample supplies for an extended siege, and hundreds of rounds of ammunition.

Over the next two hours Roberts executed five beautiful young Amish girls, wounded five others, and took his own life as police surrounded his position inside the school. The nation bore witness to these events, shocked at such violence reaching the peaceful communities of the Amish. Even more shocking was the Amish reaction.

The Amish took care of each other, as expected, visiting victims' families, preparing meals, and doing chores. But they also took care of the shooter's family. Almost immediately the Amish community established a trust fund for the Roberts family, and a stream of Amish neighbors could be seen visiting the home of Marie Roberts and other members of her family. They came not with hate and revenge, but with words of peace and forgiveness.

Ruben Fisher, grandfather of one of the slain girls, said, "It's very important that we teach the children not to think evil of the man who did this. The Roberts family has a greater load to bear than the Amish families."[3]

The Amish, living out lives of simplicity and piety, have chosen to help bear that load, to pay that price, to clear the ledger of debt, and to forgive the one who intruded upon their world and killed their children.

Thankfully, most of us will not have to face injustice of this magnitude. Few of us will be victims of a terrible crime, sold into slavery, or falsely convicted, but this does not mean we will be shielded from unjust treatment. For every high-profile transgression played out across the media, there are thousands of unspoken and unknown acts of injustice.

In bedrooms, courtrooms, and emergency rooms, far from the television cameras and investigative reports, the journey toward forgiveness or vengeance begins. Every person who has ever been violated, mistreated, cheated, or harmed—which includes everyone—will make the choice between demanding punishment or clearing the debt, between living a life of grace or a life of bitterness. These are the only two choices.

So you must choose what to do with your pain . . . the parent who abused you . . . the church leader who betrayed you . . . the corporation that stole your retirement . . . the spouse who broke your trust . . . the child who abandoned you . . . the stranger who stole something precious . . . the person who so violated you or so humiliated you that you dare not whisper it to another person.

For those who must walk this path, there are two options, forgiveness or retaliation. Some will forgive, liberating their offender and themselves.

Others will choose revenge, taking matters into their own hands or leading a life of abject bitterness.

As a young man, Yitzhak Rabin aspired to become nothing more than an irrigation engineer. In the deserts of the Middle East, where water is as valuable as oil, this was a worthy career ambition. The outbreak of World War II changed his plans and his destiny. Rabin entered the Israeli military and reached the highest levels of leadership in the young Jewish state.

Surrounded by enemies, Rabin learned to deal quickly and fiercely with his adversaries. He brilliantly engineered key military victories in the Arab-Israeli War of 1948 and the Six-Day War of 1967. Later, as defense minister, he reacted with customary harshness against Palestinian demonstrators, ordering the Israeli military to pursue a policy of "beating and breaking" the bones of Arab citizens.[4]

Throughout his career, critics and friends often accused him of belligerently pushing his nation toward war. He was quoted as saying, "You can always make peace with an F-16 in your pocket."[5]

As prime minister of Israel in the early 1990s, his second such stint, Rabin had a change of heart. He concluded that no people could be ruled by force. He candidly spoke to his nation about forsaking the siege mentality and state of war that had been so much a part of their collective identity.

He adopted the radical policy of reconciliation and peace, choosing to treat those who were once his enemies as human beings instead. Rabin entered secret negotiations with Palestinian Liberation Organization chairman Yasser Arafat to reach an agreement of peace. That agreement, now called the Oslo Accords, was officially and ceremoniously signed on the south lawn of the White House on September 13, 1993.

I was driving down the road the afternoon of the signing, and I heard Rabin's historic speech. Not wanting his words to fall to the ground, I pulled over and jotted them down on the back of a napkin. In the speech, now titled "Enough of Blood and Tears," Rabin said,

> Let me say to you, the Palestinians: We are destined to live together, on the same soil in the same land. We, the soldiers who have returned from battles stained with blood, we who have seen our relatives and friends killed before our eyes, we who have attended their funerals and cannot look into the eyes of their parents, we who have come from a land where parents bury children, we who have fought against you, the Palestinians—we say to you today in a loud and clear voice: Enough of blood and tears. Enough.

Then he said the words that so struck me that warm afternoon: "Our land is small. Our reconciliation must be great. Our wars have been long, so our peace must be sweet. . . . Deep caverns call for lofty bridges."[6]

This was a lofty bridge, a bridge that even Yitzhak Rabin had trouble walking across. When the speeches were made and the signatures placed on the document, Rabin stood facing his bitter enemy, Arafat. Rabin squirmed. He hesitated. Then, reluctantly, swallowing hard with a pucker in his brow, he took Arafat's hand in his own. He said later, "Of all the hands in the world, it was not the hand I wanted or even dreamed of touching."[7]

This valiant effort earned Rabin a share of the 1994 Nobel Peace Prize and accolades from around the world, but not everyone was happy about the course of events. Not everyone was willing to cross the lofty bridge of forgiveness.

Two years after that historical signing with Arafat, Rabin gathered with hundreds in Tel Aviv in a rally for peace, supporting the Oslo Accords. After the rally, the prime minister walked toward his waiting car. He was fired upon by one of his fellow countrymen, Yigel Amir, a young Jewish radical who so opposed peace with his neighbors that he chose to assassinate the broker of that peace. Rabin died minutes later at the Ichilov Hospital.

Fitting enough, pulled from Yitzhak Rabin's shirt pocket was a bloodstained piece of paper that recorded his last publicly spoken words, the song "Shir Lashalom"—the Song for Peace.

In part, the psalm proclaims,

Let the sun shine through again to let the flowers grow.
Don't look backward to the past; let those who left you go.
Let your eyes look up with hope, not through a rifle sight.
Sing a song, a song for love, not for another fight.
Don't tell me the day will come; work for it without cease.
It's not a dream, so inside every city square let out a cheer for peace!
Come on and sing a song for peace; don't whisper us a prayer.
Better to sing a song for peace. Let shouting fill the air![8]

Joseph laid down the weapons of revenge and by God's power embraced his brothers in forgiveness. The tears he now shed, as well as those in the future, would be tears of joy. The bitter days had finally ended. Enough blood and tears.

Questions for Reflection

1. Who are the people on your mental retaliation list? Why are they on that list? How long will you keep them there? What would it take for you to dismiss their record of wrongs?

2. Do you agree that "Every time forgiveness takes place, the price for that offense is paid, but it is paid by the victim rather than the wrongdoer"? Discuss your answer.

3. Is it possible to forgive someone and still hold a grudge? Is it possible to forgive and still want the offender to pay for what he or she has done?

4. Can someone truly forgive without God's help? Are those outside the Christian faith capable of forgiveness? Why or why not?

5. Is the Amish community being realistic in its reaction to the Nickel Mines School shooter? What effect will the Amish reaction have on the broader community? On the family of the offender? On their own children?

6. Why do some, like Yigel Amir, choose to do the hard work of unforgiveness rather than release their enemies with forgiveness?

Notes

[1] Charles Lowery, "Good Forgetters," *SBC Life* (September 1998): 16.

[2] Ron Gaynor, untitled sermon, Trinity Baptist Church, Calhoun GA, 17 October 2000.

[3] David Cox, "Grief of the Amish," *Sunday Mirror* (UK), 8 October 2006. Available online: http://findarticles.com/p/articles/mi_qn4161/is_20061008/ai_n16772181 (accessed 3 January 2008).

[4] John Conroy, *Unspeakable Acts, Ordinary People: The Dynamics of Torture* (Berkley: University of California Press, 2001), 270-71.

[5] Kevin Fedarko, "Man of Israel," *Time* 146/20 (13 November 1995), archived at http://www.time.com/time/magazine/article/0,9171,983695,00.html (accessed 18 December 2007).

[6] A complete transcript of the comments made on the occasion of the signing of the treaty can be found at in a White House press release available at http://www.historycentral.com/Documents/Clinton/ClintonSigningPLOpeace.html (accessed 13 December 2007).

[7] Fedarko.

[8] "Shir Lashalom," trans. Joel David Bloom, song by Yair Rosenbloom, 1969.

A Little Bit of Heaven

Every minute takes an hour; Every inch feels like a mile; Until I won't have to imagine; And I finally get to see you smile. — Chris Rice

In spring 2006, four Taylor University students and an employee of the school were killed in an automobile accident. The van in which they were traveling was struck by a tractor-trailer rig that had drifted out of its lane into oncoming traffic. Two of the students in the accident were Laura VanRyn and Whitney Cerak.

Whitney's family buried her following a closed-casket funeral. Laura lived, but was hospitalized with extensive injuries and remained in a coma for weeks.

As Laura began to regain consciousness, speaking a few halting words through the restriction of neck braces, broken facial bones, and horrid swelling, her family realized that something was wrong. Laura's initial conversations with her family didn't make sense. She spoke as a complete stranger. Incredibly, she was a stranger. "Laura" was not Laura at all. The VanRyn family had been caring for Whitney Cerak the entire time. In a tragic case of misidentification, the Ceraks had buried the wrong daughter.

When emergency crews arrived at the accident scene, personal identification, purses, and wallets were strewn across the highway. One of the crew mistakenly attached Laura's identification to Whitney as she was airlifted to the hospital. The two girls shared a remarkable likeness—attractive, blond, athletic—their slight differences spoiled by injuries from the accident.

A deputy coroner could have avoided this disaster had he not urged a relative to avoid looking at the body. Out of concern for the family, he felt their loss had been too much to traumatize them further.

When they realized the mistake, the VanRyns were struck with grief. Their loved one was gone. Their pain was balanced by the Ceraks' shock and joy. Having buried their daughter, granddaughter, and sister, the Ceraks essentially received her back from the dead. Whitney's funeral, attended by more than a thousand people, had been unwarranted.

The tombstone, with her name already etched in the marble, was removed from the cemetery. She who was dead was made alive again. Whitney's grandfather, Emil Frank, said news of his granddaughter's survival was staggering beyond belief. "I still can't get over it," he said. "It's like a fairytale."[1]

Jacob must have felt like he had awakened in a make-believe world as his sons returned from Egypt with the news that Joseph was alive. He had sent them to get grain. They brought home word of a long-lost son. Joseph had been dead to Jacob for twenty-two years. Eight thousand days and nights. This was more than a reunion. It was a resurrection.

> And they left Egypt and returned to their father, Jacob, in the land of Canaan.
>
> "Joseph is still alive!" they told him. "And he is governor of all the land of Egypt!" Jacob was stunned at the news—he couldn't believe it. But when they repeated to Jacob everything Joseph had told them, and when he saw the wagons Joseph had sent to carry him, their father's spirits revived.
>
> Then Jacob exclaimed, "It must be true! My son Joseph is alive! I must go and see him before I die." (Gen 45:25-28)

The Hebrew text of the breaking of the news is more telling than our English translation. The New Living Translation above says Jacob was "stunned" by the news. The King James Version comes a little closer to the original Hebrew, stating that "Jacob's heart fainted." Literally, Jacob's heart went cold.

The news, good news though it was, came perilously close to taking Jacob's life. At 130 years old, his old frail body could barely take the excitement. But Jacob rallied his fluttering heart for the chance at seeing Joseph again. After being separated for so long, nothing would stop Jacob from being with his son, not even a long, difficult, dusty trip through the desert riding in a borrowed ox cart.

Having served as a church pastor and a hospital chaplain, I have been astounded at the formidable strength of the old and sick at the time of death. Whether it is with a loved parishioner from my own church or a stranger admitted into the hospital's intensive care unit, I have kept vigil with grieving family members, waiting for death to arrive.

Lingering in the darkness of a hospital room I have watched vital signs decline to nearly nothing. Breathing grows shallow. Hands are held. Brows are wiped. Prayers are offered. Tears are shed.

Still, the loved one, reduced to bruised flesh and shrunken bones, holds on to life. "How is this possible?" I often wonder. In many cases the sufferer is waiting—not for death—but for a loved one to arrive.

A beloved daughter at long last enters the hospital room; or a son, having crossed multiple time zones, finally arrives at the bedside; or a childhood friend makes that closing visit. Then, and only then, is the Herculean grip on life released. Such is the power of reunion.

This prospect of such a reunion—the thought of seeing Joseph's face one last time—was enough to carry Jacob out of the Promised Land to Egypt. Tyron Edwards said, "Every parting is a form of death, [and] every reunion is a type of heaven."[2] Jacob looked forward to a little heaven on earth.

Heaven. It is an archaic subject these days. As a child growing up in the impoverished hills of lower Appalachia, I found that heaven was a constant theme in our church worship services. The old-timers at church—skinny little men in overalls and blue-haired ladies dressed in floral prints—spoke of heaven as if they had actually been there. The streets of gold, the pearly gates, the celestial city: they spoke of these with such descriptive detail and aching passion that I could envision it all in my mind.

Cheeks would glisten with tears as feeble hands were raised in thanksgiving to God. Occasionally, if the Spirit blew just right and the sermon was focused on the sweet forever, some of these erstwhile church veterans would shout for joy to a chorus of "Amens" and "Hallelujahs," startling the preacher and causing near heart failure in children like me.

One morning not long ago I was in a local coffee house enjoying my coffee and spending time in front of my laptop. Two gentlemen planted themselves at a small table next to me. I wasn't intentionally eavesdropping on their conversation, but they were speaking so loudly and so unguardedly that I heard every word.

They chatted about their work, the weather, their golf games, and finally settled on the topic of the miserable state of the world. Before leaving one said, "I wish Jesus would just come back today and get us out of here. Then everybody left behind would have to sort this mess out." This statement was followed by a near gleeful exchange about God's coming judgment on the world.

When they finally left my coffee had turned cold. So had my heart. It was not so much their eschatology, that is, their beliefs about the end of the world, that chilled me. I have been familiar with their rapturous ambitions since my childhood, drinking it down with my mother's milk. It was their hoped-for escapism and stark abandonment of God's creation that made me shiver.

Their solution, put in post-Hurricane Katrina terms, was an air rescue. Thousands—millions—drown in rising despair, but a few are snatched from the rooftops at the critical moment. Those unfortunate enough not to catch a ride are abandoned to divine retribution. Maybe it was the cavalier manner the men discussed such weighty things that contributed to my unease. The Apocalypse was handled with the same relaxed tone as tomorrow's weather forecast. How could this be? How could the destruction of the universe be spoken of with anything resembling delight? I suppose it's difficult to give a damn about the world, or the people in it, when our greatest hope is to escape it.

Christ entered the world, we Christians believe, as God in the flesh come to pierce creation with the hope of the kingdom of heaven. His message was not about escaping to paradise per se, letting the chips fall where they may. It was about living out that redemptive kingdom *now*. When his contemporaries rejected this hope, Christ was struck with bitter weeping. His heart broke into pieces. When Jesus looked out at the multitude of miserable peasants, abusive religionists, and corrupt governments of his day, he didn't see targets for God's judgment. He saw vulnerable sheep without a shepherd. Christ was up to his eyeballs engaging the culture, not hoping for its destruction.

My elders' preoccupation with paradise was not driven by this kind of calloused coffee shop escapism. Having endured the hardships of poverty, war, sickness, and loss, they considered heaven a definite step up, an eternal reprieve from the madness of the world; but it was not an escape hatch these dear ones wanted.

What they desired was not heaven itself, but to be with their loved ones already there. Those who spoke of heaven with the greatest affection could not care less about mansions or angels or metallic streets. These were peripheral benefits at best.

What their hearts yearned for—what their hearts broke for—was reunion. "Jordon's Stormy Banks" were a welcome destination on the journey that would carry them into the arms of a spouse, a child, or a parent who had passed over years before. If the heart is truly found where we have placed our treasure, as Jesus said, then those who have loved ones in heaven have already sent their hearts ahead.

What is heaven? In large part, it is that place where loved ones are reunited, where relationships are restored, where all that has gone wrong between people will be made right. Heaven is the final destination of all creation, as God will once again make everything as he first created it. It will all be good. Who cannot long for a place like that? Who cannot find themselves drawn to such a paradise? Why wait?

As the mercy of Christ makes our entry into his kingdom of restoration possible, where we will be with those from whom we have been separated, so forgiveness opens the door for this same kind of renewal now. Heaven is possible on earth. We get a taste of it every time forgiveness and reconciliation take place.

My wife and I have friends who suffered difficult days in their marriage. The wife, Terri, called me with a broken heart and a question.

"Ronnie, have you heard what Chris has done?"

Her voice was weak and squishy, the consequence of having cried all night I suppose. Terri didn't have to say another word. I knew exactly what Chris had done.

Recently, Chris had intimated to me struggles of faith. I was concerned not because he was struggling; we all do that. I was concerned because, knowing Chris well, I knew I wasn't getting the whole story. Something was going on behind the scenes, and I knew it the way close friends know what they know about each other.

I finally pressed Chris and he confided that his marriage, from his perspective, was in dire straits. For years there had been a seething resentment between his wife and him over issues unresolved since the earliest days of their relationship. Poor communication, emotional upheaval, misunderstandings—all the usual suspects were in his home. Now, three children and years later, Chris was calling it quits. In the bed of another woman he had found the emotional solace he always seemed to lack.

"Why won't God change Chris's mind?" Terri asked.

"That's not God's way," I countered.

"Why isn't God keeping his promises?" she wondered.

"But he has," I answered.

"No he hasn't! I'm headed toward a divorce!" she said.

"Chris has broken his promise, Terri, not God."

Terri finally reached the reason for her call: "Will you call him and talk some sense into him?"

I was silent. For almost a minute, an eternity within a telephone conversation, I said nothing but listened to Terri's crying. When the silence became unbearable, she asked again, "Will you talk to him?"

Truthfully, I had tried to talk to Chris for weeks to no avail. He was avoiding me. I promised this grieving wife that, yes, I would hunt him down and talk to him.

Then I added, "Terri, understand that my words will be mostly powerless. He has made up his mind and only time, the outcome of his decision, and God himself can change things now."

"How long should I wait, then?" she asked.

"There's no timetable for such things," I answered. "I wish I had the ability to take you a year, five years, a decade into the future and let you see the person you will be—healed, whole, breathing deeply the grace of God—with or without Chris. That day will come, though you can't believe it now. And when it does, we'll smile and remember this conversation today."

That day did come. Chris and Terri reconciled, though not without many tears and great difficulty, and we all celebrated in the aftermath. Forgiveness—on both sides—made it possible for these two to be together again. That is very good. That is heaven, no matter which way you look at it.

Sometimes heaven doesn't seem to arrive on earth. The offending party dies or moves away. One or more persons in a conflict have no desire to reconcile or even attempt to make things right. Barriers beyond our control are put in the way of resolution. What then? Is "one-sided" forgiveness possible? Absolutely.

Joseph's forgiveness of his brothers did not depend upon their attitude, reaction, or commitment to restoration. He could and did forgive regardless of how those who had hurt him responded. There is a therapeutic nature to forgiveness that reaches past the offender and back into the heart of the one offended. Forgiveness sets the criminal free, yes, but more so, it sets free the one who has been mistreated or hurt.

When we grant forgiveness to others we turn the key, open the door, and exit the jail cell of our own imprisonment. We escape future bitterness and resentment. We cut loose the chains and weight of condemnation—ours and theirs. We are delivered from carrying around the heavy burden of holding others responsible and punishable for their actions.

The authors of *The Critical Journey* make this point with an articulate retelling from the movie *The Mission*. A priest assigns penance to a former slave trader for his many sins. To help him with his atonement, the priest goes with the slaver as he was to

> . . . carry a heavy burden strapped to his back to a village accessible only by climbing a gigantic waterfall. After an arduous, treacherous, and exhausting climb with the priest, they finally arrived at the top of the waterfall. There they were greeted joyously by relatives of the villagers the slaver had previously kidnapped and sold into slavery.
>
> One young man recognized the once feared and hated slaver. He stepped forward and then graciously cut the burden loose from his back. The slaver broke down in a flood of tears. The simple relief and the acceptance of forgiveness . . . were overwhelming.[3]

While reconciliation of relationships may involve more than you personally—it takes two to reconcile—it only takes you to forgive. That forgiveness is good for you, good for others, and may lead to even greater restoration.

Be reminded of this, however: The forgiveness and reconciliation extended by Joseph to his family did not materialize overnight. He did not follow a prefabricated "three-step plan" of forgiveness that came wrapped in a neat little box after he attended a weekend retreat. This miracle of grace germinated for many years, over more than two decades, before it began to bloom and bear fruit. But what beautiful fruit it was in the end:

> As they neared their destination, Jacob sent Judah ahead to meet Joseph and get directions to the region of Goshen. And when they finally arrived there, Joseph prepared his chariot and traveled to Goshen to meet his father, Jacob. When Joseph arrived, he embraced his father and wept, holding him for a long time.
>
> Finally, Jacob said to Joseph, "Now I am ready to die, since I have seen your face again and know you are still alive." (Gen 46:28-30)

Think of it: If Joseph hadn't forgiven his brothers, what would have happened to this family? Possibly, Joseph's brothers, their wives, and children would have died of starvation in Palestine. Or perhaps Joseph would have exterminated them in anger and they would have never returned home. Jacob, old and heartbroken, would have gone to the grave deprived of all his children, not just one. In the redemptive narrative of God, the family of promise—the family that would incubate and eventually produce the Messiah, the Christ—would have faded into the obscurity of history.

Forgiveness short-circuited these disasters and kept the promise of a future alive for the family of Jacob. Ultimately, Joseph's forgiveness kept this promise alive for us all.

Questions for Reflection

1. Have you ever been with a dying loved one who seemed to be waiting for something to happen or someone to arrive? What was it like?

2. Not long ago, many Christians spoke of heaven warmly and often. Why do Christians seem to speak less of it now? Do you think heaven is an overdeveloped or underdeveloped hope in the church today?

3. The man at the coffee shop told his friend, "I wish Jesus would just come back today and get us out of here. Then everybody left behind would have to sort this mess out." Is this a common attitude among Christians today? Is there anything wrong with this kind of thinking? If so, what?

4. Should Christians be more concerned with preparing themselves for heaven or living for Christ now? Why?

5. Forgiveness was as liberating for Joseph as it was for his brothers. Who receives the most benefit in the process of forgiveness: the offended or the offender?

6. Why do you think Joseph ultimately forgave his brothers? For his own sake? For the sake of his father? For Benjamin?

Notes

[1] James Prichard, "Mistake ID Stuns Crash Victims' Families," *Associated Press*, 1 June 2006.

[2] Adam Woolever, *Treasure of Wisdom, Wit and Humor, Odd Comparisons and Proverbs* (Philadelphia: David McKay, 1891), 309.

[3] Robert A. Guelich and Janet O. Hagberg, *The Critical Journey, Stages in the Life of Faith*, 2nd ed. (Salem WI: Sheffield Publishing, 2004), 36.

But God Meant It for Good

Accept the place divine Providence has found for you.

— *Ralph Waldo Emerson*

In summer 1998 I visited the Fort Knox gold mine operated by the Kinross Corporation. This open pit is located just north of Fairbanks, Alaska, and it is the largest gold-mining operation in North America. While gold has been enticed from the Fairbanks mining district for a hundred years, no one has drilled, blasted, and processed with the immense efficiency found at Fort Knox.

The mine covers more than 50,000 acres of the Alaskan wilderness. Haul trucks the size of suburban homes move more than 100,000 tons of material every day. The mill, adjacent to this massive hole in the ground, refines the material 365 days a year, 7 days a week, 24 hours a day. The operation never rests.

The process amazed me. Rock blasted from the earth is dumped onto conveyor belts that feed the never-ending hunger of the mill. Once inside, the rock is mashed inside a gyrating crusher. From there it is tumbled into even smaller pieces through a series of machines that resemble the inner workings of a large Laundromat.

Ultimately the ore and rock are reduced to a thick gumbo that sits in leach tanks, mixing and interacting with lead nitrate, cyanide, and other chemicals that draw the gold out of the sludge. This final product is melted down into bars and shipped, under heavy guard, to refineries.

The process is time consuming, tedious, and expensive. The Kinross Corporation must process thirty-three tons of material to produce a single ounce of sellable gold. In other words, the one small wedding ring on your left hand had to be wrung out of enough rock to match the size and weight of the Statue of Liberty. For all the effort, the finished product is apparently worth it.

My reading of Peter's first epistle has taken on a deeper meaning in light of this visit to the Alaskan boondocks. Peter writes,

> So be truly glad. There is wonderful joy ahead, even though you have to endure many trials for a little while. These trials will show that your faith is genuine. It is being tested as fire tests and purifies gold—though your faith is far more precious than mere gold. So when your faith remains strong through many trials, it will bring you much praise and glory and honor on the day when Jesus Christ is revealed to the whole world. (1 Pet 1:6-7)

The fire of today's gold refineries burns with ruthless chemical precision. The recovery rate, the percentage of actual ore retrieved from the earth's crust, is 90 percent. Very little of what shines is allowed to remain hidden beneath the soil. The metal is too precious, too valuable, too important to be left behind.

God feels the same way about you. We enter the world as a heap of flint-like stone with hard edges and an unprocessed, wayward heart. God, using the circumstances of life, family, good and bad decisions, begins to pulverize our rocky hearts. Over time we are broken, gyrated, tumbled, and burned. It feels like there is nothing left to us but sludge.

It is then that God is doing his greatest work. For when the pain is most intense, the healing and reconstructing are most evident. When the refining fires are at their hottest, God's grace is at its best.

There, deep within us, gleaming like twenty-four-carat gold, is a purified and sparkling faith; a faith we did not even know we possessed; a faith that would have gone otherwise unknown and unseen without the flames of adversity. God considers this a treasure too important to leave in the dirt.

Joseph's life began with little noticeable value. He was an insignificant player, a child in the backwoods of Palestine. Spoiled, pampered, and condescending, he didn't possess many redeeming qualities, but God saw a sparkle beneath the surface. Through the furnaces of betrayal, injustice, and abandonment, Joseph came out the other side with more than experience. He emerged with character, strength, and a faith in the God who always works things according to his good will.

One of my mentors, Horace Stewart, has spent his ministry as a pastor, chaplain, and mental health professional. Often he shares this simple word of counsel with those who are in the midst of great difficulty: "Don't waste it."

He shared those words with me once. Puzzled, I asked him what he could possibly mean. He said, "When life is hard, God is up to something. Don't miss it. Don't waste it." I'm now thankful for those words.

This is the answer Joseph gave his brothers to explain his own life. The adversity had not been a squandering of time or life, but an intentional, purposeful process.

> After burying Jacob, Joseph returned to Egypt with his brothers and all who had accompanied him to his father's burial. But now that their father was dead, Joseph's brothers became fearful. "Now Joseph will show his anger and pay us back for all the wrong we did to him," they said.
>
> So they sent this message to Joseph: "Before your father died, he instructed us to say to you: 'Please forgive your brothers for the great wrong they did to you—for their sin in treating you so cruelly.' So we, the servants of the God of your father, beg you to forgive our sin." When Joseph received the message, he broke down and wept. Then his brothers came and threw themselves down before Joseph. "Look, we are your slaves!" they said.
>
> But Joseph replied, "Don't be afraid of me. Am I God, that I can punish you? You intended to harm me, but God intended it all for good. He brought me to this position so I could save the lives of many people. No, don't be afraid. I will continue to take care of you and your children." So he reassured them by speaking kindly to them. (Gen 50:14-21)

Joseph's brothers had a legitimate fear: Would Joseph's goodness toward them last any longer than their father? With Jacob now buried, what would become of them? Has Joseph merely tolerated them for the sake of the old man, only to punish them now that the patriarch had been gathered to his ancestors?

They fell once again on their faces before Joseph. As the book of Genesis draws to a close, this is the last place we find them—fulfilling a final time Joseph's legendary dreams.

Joseph's forgiveness, however, was not temporary. The fears of his former betrayers moved him to tears. He embraced his brothers anew, providing them an explanation for their actions—his own complicated life and the God-given ability to forgive.

Joseph understood his life to be part of an extensive, divine design in which his sufferings played a significant role. The injustice suffered at the hands of his brothers was God's means of ultimately saving their entire family. Joseph journeyed through a nightmarish storm only to arrive at the conclusion that, yes, God had truly meant it all for good.

This day in the palace, following the burial of his father, was not the first time Joseph articulated this reasoning for the experiences of his life. Back in Genesis 45, where Joseph first identifies himself as the long-lost brother, he uses the phrase, "You sold me," speaking of his brothers, interchangeably with the phrase, "God sent me." In Joseph's thinking these two expressions were impossible to separate.

Yes, the brothers made the conscious decision to harm their youngest brother by selling him into slavery and then covering their sin with the pretense of an animal attack. At the same time, though, God opportunely used these events to bring about a greater good for all involved.

This intersection between human decision and divine providence, so well illustrated in the ancient narrative of Joseph, has been debated, systemized, and squabbled over for most of Christian history. How is it possible for individual freedom and God's sovereignty to be somehow reconciled?

A. W. Tozer provides a hackneyed but valuable example. He writes,

An ocean liner leaves New York bound for Liverpool. Its destination has been determined by proper authorities. Nothing can change it. This is at least a faint picture of sovereignty. On board the liner are several scores of passengers. These are not in chains, neither are their activities determined for them by decree. They are completely free to move about as they will. They eat, sleep, play, lounge about on the deck, read, talk, altogether as they please; but all the while the great liner is carrying them steadily onward toward a predetermined port.

Both freedom and sovereignty are present here and they do not contradict each other. So it is, I believe, with man's freedom and the sovereignty of God. The mighty liner of God's sovereign design keeps its steady course over the sea of history. God moves undisturbed and unhindered toward the fulfilment [sic] of those eternal purposes which He purposed in Christ Jesus before the world began. We do not know all that is included in those purposes, but enough has been disclosed to furnish us with a broad outline of things to come and to give us good hope and firm assurance of future well-being.[1]

A contemporary illustration comes from the pen of Brian McLaren. Writing about the Lord's Prayer, and particularly the request within that prayer, "Thy will be done," McLaren notes,

> "The will of God" can evoke the idea of a despot, a tyrant, a puppeteer, a deterministic machine operator imposing his will, turning a prayer for liberation into a plea for an end to free will. (Of course, if God were such a controlling God, it's hard to imagine how such a prayer would ever become necessary in the first place!) Since the language of "will" can take us down a trail of control, domination, and coercion, and since I don't believe those ideas are in Jesus' mind at all, I have looked for other words.
>
> The Greek word that lies beneath our English word "will" can also be translated "wish." But to say, "May your wish come true" sounds rather fairy tale-ish and creates other problems. But I have found the idea of "the dream of God for creation" does the job quite nicely. "Your kingdom come, your will be done on earth as it is in heaven" could thus be rendered "May all your dreams for your creation come true." This language suggests a more personal, less mechanistic relationship between God and our world. It would resonate, for example, with a mother who has great dreams for her child, or a coach who has great dreams for her team, or an artist who has great dreams for a novel or painting or symphony he is creating, or a teacher who has high dreams for his students . . . .
>
> This metaphor also gives us a responsible and creative role to play. . . . The call to faith is the call to trust God and God's dreams enough to realign our dreams with God's, to dream our little dreams within God's big dream . . . to continually receive God's dreams . . . to publicly identify with God's dream and to disassociate with all competing -isms or ideologies that claim to provide the ultimate dream . . . [and] to learn to live the way God dreams for us all to live.[2]

Clearly Joseph's dreams were more than messages from God. They were God's dreams for the future. Joseph was satisfied to play his vital part in this divine drama. Joseph endured. Joseph forgave. Joseph extended grace. Joseph learned well in the classroom of adversity and joined with God in a bright and redemptive future. It was this recognition of God's dreamful intentions that gave Joseph hope.

When Joseph was being dragged in chains across the Sinai desert, a dreamful hope buoyed his spirits. When his hands bled with the work of slavery and he cried for home in the dark Egyptian night, hope met him with each new morning. When he lay on a prison cot feeling his youth slip away with each day, this hope of a future kept him alive.

As he stood in his palace with the phantoms of the past bowing before him, it was still hope—hope produced by God's well-intended purpose—that enabled Joseph to forgive. Joseph understood that hope was active in his life in spite of the injustices that threatened to snuff him out.

It has been rightly observed that we human beings need precious few essentials in order to survive: Food—without it, we will starve in four to six weeks. Water—even more crucial, the body's systems are crippled without it in only three days. Air—it takes only seven minutes before brain damage is irreversible. And hope—no one can live, truly live, a second without it.

Hope is the intangible fuel that moves the human spirit along when life appears, well, hopeless. When marriages fail, when sickness invades, when relationships crumble, when our finances collapse, it is then that we anticipate—we hope—that somehow conditions will improve. We hope that tomorrow will be brighter. We hope that the future will be different than the present.

Hope enables us to face whatever difficulties come our way with a greater measure of resolve. If that hope is taken away, our spirits wilt and resistance fades. We need hope to live in this world the same way we need oxygen in our lungs.

Hope, in the end, is not an impossible dream. "God intended it all for good" is more than Joseph's song. It is a song that can be sung by us all. We only must listen for the melody of God's grace and faithfulness, understanding that we are not the only ones dreaming of a world where all things work together for our good. God dreams and plans and works for that world as well.

Joseph not only lived off this hope, but he also left it to his family. As the book of Genesis comes to a close, Joseph gathers his brothers and their families and his own immediate family to himself for final words.

Lying on his deathbed he says to them,

> "Soon I will die," Joseph told his brothers, "but God will surely come to help you and lead you out of this land of Egypt. He will bring you back to the land he solemnly promised to give to Abraham, to Isaac, and to Jacob."
>
> Then Joseph made the sons of Israel swear an oath, and he said, "When God comes to help you and lead you back, you must take my bones with you." So Joseph died at the age of 110. The Egyptians embalmed him, and his body was placed in a coffin in Egypt. (Gen 50:24-26)

Joseph lived long enough to see changes on the Egyptian landscape. He understood what was coming. When he was a young man, his foresight, planning, and execution had saved the country from certain starvation. Now old, crippled, and marginal, he was a has-been.

His heroics were forgotten, and soon Egypt's gratitude toward the Hebrews would be replaced with animosity, suspicion, and slavery. Joseph, a final time, seemed to be the only one who could see the future. His counsel for these uncertain days was to trust the same God who had brought him through the difficulties of life.

The descendants of Israel would now experience exactly what Joseph had endured. They would be enslaved in a foreign country. They would be wrongly exploited and put in chains. They would be forgotten in the dungeons and deserts of Egypt. They would suffer unmercifully through no fault of their own.

Finally, though, hope and faith would become sight. A deliverer would come, and when the people of Israel left the land of Egypt to return home, they would carry the bones, hope, and faith of Joseph with them.

My prayer is that you will carry this same faith with you on your journey. People, even those friends closest to you, will let you down. Family members will deceive you. Faith communities, organizations, and employers will betray you. Life will dishearten you. Believe it or not, even your own abilities will fail you. All of these, given time, will disappoint, but through it all, he who calls us will remain faithful.

This is more than a dream. This is the promise of God.

Questions for Reflection

1. God's work in our lives could be compared to that of a gold refinery. Have you ever felt like there was "nothing left to you but sludge"? At the time, did you have any sense of God's activity in your life?

2. Would Joseph have turned out to be a man of faith and character without his trials in Egypt? Why or why not?

3. Scripture tells us, "So they sent this message to Joseph: 'Before your father died, he instructed us to say to you: 'Please forgive your brothers for the great wrong they did to you—for their sin in treating you so cruelly.' So we, the servants of the God of your father, beg you to forgive our sin.'" This is an obvious lie after Jacob's death. Have Joseph's brothers actually changed? Why would they lie like this?

4. Joseph could not separate "You sold me," speaking of his brothers, from the statement "God sent me." Can these two be separated? Did God cause Joseph's brothers to sell him into Egypt?

5. Brian McLaren speaks of the will of God as the "dream of God." Is this a good choice of words? Are there dangers of speaking of God's will as God's "dream"? If so, what are these dangers?

6. Joseph's story is a foreshadowing of the story of the Hebrew people who would be enslaved in Egypt. Do you think Joseph's story was recorded for their benefit or some other reason?

Notes

[1] A. W. Tozer, *The Knowledge of the Holy*, reissue ed. (New York: HarperSanFrancisco, 1978), 118.

[2] Brian McLaren, *The Secret Message of Jesus: Uncovering the Truth that Could Change Everything* (Nashville: W Publishing Group, 2006), 140-42.